THE FOUR FITS
OF DYNAMIC LEADERSHIP

THE FOUR FITS
OF DYNAMIC LEADERSHIP

Dr. Terrence D. Duncan and
CMSGT (Ret.) Walter Duncan, Jr.

ISBN: 1545250391
ISBN 13: 9781545250396
Library of Congress Control Number: 2017905654
CreateSpace Independent Publishing Platform
North Charleston, South Carolina

TABLE OF CONTENTS

The Four Fits of Dynamic Leadership

Acknowledgment and Dedication

I DEDICATE THIS book to my father, U.S. Air Force Chief Master Sergeant (Ret.) Walter Duncan, Jr., who passed away on January 11, 2017. Not only did he serve his country with honor, but he was also a natural leader who overcame adversity in his personal and professional life. Even though the statistics were against him from day one, he never stopped and always persevered. He checked off all the boxes that he wanted to accomplish during his time on this Earth.

I give him credit for this book because I watched him and remember the moments of frustrations and triumphs as a child, and as an independent man of my own. Despite his subject matter expertise, he was also able to blend his personality and self-awareness with his team. At his funeral, many of his coworkers from the military to the judiciary, as well as friends far and away came to pay respect to this proud, caring, and giving man who left us too soon at the age of 61. Despite passing away at an early age, he leaves behind riches of memories, conversations, and advice that have helped shape into the man that I am today. I wrote approximately 90% of this book before his passing. It is only appropriate that I complete this book, and give him credit for all that his style of leadership and compassion that permeates throughout this book.

Therefore, for every copy provided, his name and his mark will forever be available for those to read and dissect, as he is with me always. I love you and will always miss you, Dad.

INTRODUCTION

The Four Fits of Dynamic Leadership

IF YOU ASKED numerous business leaders, CEOs, CFOs, and managers, you would likely receive several different definitions of leadership. Despite different definitions of what defines leadership, each is correct. The administration of leadership varies based on the individual's perceptions, biases, beliefs, morals, and values. Leadership is an intangible entity that empowers yourself and others around you to reach a shared vision or goal.

Loyalty and turnover affect the ability to manage assets properly. Staff tends to leave for a variety of reasons, as more options become available to them. With the advent of eroding pensions, contributions to 401k, and limited raises, the typical staff member, referred to as associates interchangeably throughout the book, may seek other means to reach his or her personal goals and aspirations. The challenge of leadership today, and likely for years to come, is to understand how to align with the desires and wants of their staff.

If you are currently in a managerial or executive level position, recall your ascension to your current position. Remember the numerous hours you spent contemplating your future. You may be one who aspired to reach a certain pinnacle of management. You may be one who dreamed about running a division or an entire organization. Possibly, you are not in a management position or an executive level position, but you seek and desire to be there one day. Your aspirations, dreams, and ambition make up the inner dynamic core of your motivation to reach certain heights. No matter your current position or desired position, you started from somewhere.

I realized that to improve; I had to change. Every day when I wake up, no matter what is on my mind, I have to possess the will to change something from within whether it is a mode of thinking or challenging myself to become better than the day before. I challenge you to ask yourself, if you want to be a leader, how can anyone follow you if you choose to be complacent?

Leadership is something you can develop over the course of time. When you started your college courses, you probably found yourself admiring or following another person who demonstrated characteristics of leadership or had a large following. For those who have a love of sports, you may see someone become more of a leader over the course of his or her career.

Understanding that developing leadership from within is part of your overall growth. Understand that leadership does not have to be particularly related to Corporate America or managerial titles. Simply because you are in charge by title, does not mean that you are in charge by example. Leadership comes from within. Leadership is not a given. Leadership comes from respect, not through cajoling or dictating.

In my first book, *The Four Fits of Holistic Growth,* I explored the concept of personal motivation and personal development from within. Philosophically, I believed that we should refrain from living in a box. The way we should attempt to live our lives should not be divided into quarters or in a matrix. Instead, the Four Fits provided an opportunity to grow exponentially from developing four key areas: Spiritual/Mental Fit, Emotional Fit, Financial Fit, and Physical Fit. The book required the reader to look internally in an honest and open fashion to connect the dots in a non-linear fashion. By learning how to develop from within and without boundaries, the reader developed a holistic mentality.

Conceptually, *The Four Fits of Holistic Growth* did not add anything significantly new to the discussions of personal development, motivation, and self-awareness. Instead, the book provided a realistic mindset to practical problems that most people commonly encounter. There may never be a complete playbook in life, as we face numerous scenarios that require us to adapt to that situation and use our instincts and prior experiences to overcome these obstacles. However, the intent and purpose of the book were to help develop the mindset to become more focused on how to address each barrier with your mind, body, spirit, and soul being in sync.

This book borrows from some of the core themes from its counterpart and includes it under the leadership and management dynamic. If you went to a bookstore or checked your preferred e-reader, you will see numerous books, blogs, and topics related to leadership and management. Some are more thoughtful and more insightful than others. Some resemble a 200-level undergraduate course. Although there is no correct formula in discussing leadership and management principles, this book attempts to provide a dynamic and holistic approach towards leadership.

In parts of this book, you will find discussions from a managerial perspective. I cannot reasonably assume that everyone who is reading this book is currently in a position of management. Therefore, I attempt to write this book from a broad outlook based on my numerous personal and professional experiences. These experiences help shape my ideology, as well as various interactions with clients, co-workers, and associates who work directly and indirectly under my leadership and tutelage.

The purpose of this book is to have you embrace these examples, interactions, and scenarios that I have observed, encountered, or others have experienced in the workplace. Even though leadership is not limited to one setting, industry, or occupation, the basis for most of the stories and guidance throughout the book will center around a healthcare setting. Most environments are similar to healthcare settings in that there are multiple stakeholders, internal and external. In healthcare settings, and like other industry organizational structures, you have multiple divisions working in concert to achieve the same set of goals and principles. Also, in a healthcare setting, different skill sets are brought into play, and the challenge of any organization is to understand how to channel all those skills into a common goal or goals to be achieved daily.

As I imagine other readers of this book are from different industries, titles, and experiences, I believe that this book has interchangeable aspects that are fitting for you and your organizational strategy.

Similar to *The Four Fits of Holistic Growth*, this book is a conversation rich with a mindset full of an outside the box mentality. The anecdotes provided within the book, provide a foundation to build upon as the psyche of the modern worker continues to evolve. This book is not limited to the workplace setting. If you are a person seeking to lead an organization, committee, or movement, this book is beneficial for you as well.

Being dynamic means that you are more than ordinary. Being dynamic means that you are willing to take a different outlook and approach to situations or obstacles presented. Being dynamic is to become captivating by demonstrating how you can be in charge regardless of your experiences, job title, or current position in a typical hierarchal organizational chart. Being dynamic starts with you being you. It is my hope that this contribution towards the exhaustive amount of literature provided throughout decades of work brings some new energy, thoughtfulness, and a new perspective in becoming an energetic and dynamic leader willing to bring about change.

CHAPTER 1

WHAT ARE THE FOUR FITS OF DYNAMIC LEADERSHIP?

THE FOUR FITS of Dynamic Leadership is a philosophy I developed that combines the spirit, energy, and compassion that lies within you and channeling it towards your ability to lead, motivate, encourage, and excite. Your capacity to lead and to capture the spirit of those around you provide you the capability to improve production, meet core values and goals, and better dictate your mission. I firmly believe the more dynamic you are as a person, the more you are willing to show the multiple dimensions of your personality and being, all the while staying true to yourself, you have unlimited potential to tap into the essence of those around you.

You still play a significant role in your organization, which you must always remember that; however, you are not a robot. Your management style may be efficient 15 – 20 years ago; however, the responsiveness from your associates may not be as receptive as you had hoped it to be. We must realize and embrace the changes that occurred in the world during the past decade or so. We must further understand that change is inevitable. Despite change being inevitable, we must take comfort that most changes have purpose meaning, and value for you and those around you.

Resistance to change may have detrimental effects on your ability to lead. Refusing to take heed of the winds of change and sticking firm to the old ways may cause you to miss opportunities which are beneficial to you and your organization. Resistance to change creates difficulty in communication, a disjointed message from core leadership, potential for misunderstanding between staff and management, and potential for internal chaos. Recognizing the barriers of change benefits the organization by removing obstacles, whether physical or mental, from core organizational objectives.

Most associates in the workplace work with a certain level of comfort. They understand what their primary role may be, and this provides some degree of productivity. If an organization enacts a new concept, procedure, or protocol, change occurs. As a leader, if you accept change, the implementation process may go more smoothly if you demonstrate a willingness to embrace it. If you are resistant to change and attempt to enact the change or motivate your associates to transition from comfortable and known practices, the innovation and its purpose become lost.

A challenge for those administering the change is the willingness to accept innovation without much question or delay. If the leaders implementing the innovative change through an organization remains locked under a command and control leadership, the change and the process become more complicated and arduous (Plsek & Wilson, 2001). The best type of innovation develops without the natural tendency to be resistant to change. The benefits of the innovation do not materialize if resistance continues to permeate from those responsible implementing change.

The concepts of the Four Fits of Dynamic Leadership embrace change and change agents. Most leadership models use a matrix model to describe how leaders and management should move. Under the Four Fits concept, the model used encompasses a sphere. Take a pen and a piece of paper, draw a circle, and think about what you are seeking. You see that the circle is a sphere, it is round. If you made that circle three-dimensional, potential for movement within that sphere exists. If you were capable of animating objects within the circle, those objects are capable of moving freely without constraints or boundaries.

The philosophy of the Four Fits I designed for personal motivation, personal development, self-awareness, and leadership are similar in that you are permitted to move freely within your thought process without being locked in a particular matrix, box, or zone. Under the Four Fits, your movement is defined by whatever means you desire. You are allowed to blend a mix of one Fit with another, as each Fit is interchangeable and interrelated. To illustrate the Four Fits concepts, I have provided a matrix and a sphere to review:

Table 1: Four Fits of Holistic Growth in Matrix Form

Mental Fit	Emotional Fit
Team Fit	Personal Power Fit

As you observe the matrix form of The Four Fits, you notice the lines that exist within the matrix. This form of the model is restrictive. The model represents a box that is closed-ended and limited. Although it is possible to move from one segment to another, you are somewhat limited in quadrants. Quadrants represent a linearity and rigidness that are not conducive to becoming a dynamic leader. As you continue to read what each Fit serves with its related worksheets, I encourage you to continue to come back to this model to gain a better understanding as to the linearity and rigidness of this particular model.

Table 2: Four Fits of Dynamic Leadership True Model

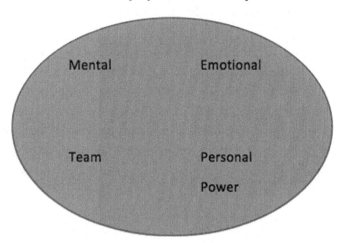

The spherical model of the Four Fits is more appropriate for this philosophical context as there are no lines that create barriers to your movement within the sphere. Within this model, you are capable of interchanging your position within the sphere, as well as providing the unlimited potential to add within the sphere. Some may be more invested in the Emotional Fit than the Personal Power Fit. Some may be more invested in the Mental Fit than the Team Fit; however, under both circumstances, you are still capable of drawing from within each Fit and incorporating it under your biggest strengths. The benefit of this model provides you the opportunity to become more abstract, multi-dimensional, and dynamic.

Demonstrating flexibility is a fundamental component of leadership. We often develop visions and plans under the assumption that if everything works out in a way that we desire, we will reach our achieved objective or goal with limited disruptions. Unfortunately, there are not too many situations where this frame of thinking applies. We often encounter events, situations, and game-changing moments where a critical decision is needed. Before making this decision, we are not certain if the path that we select will be the correct one. Despite this unknown variable, we still must make a decision and must demonstrate the capability to adjust and adapt.

Use of the Four Fits concept provides you the flexibility you need regardless of the industry, company, organization, or project. Drawing on these unique and dynamic aspects of the Fits helps create a balance necessary to lead and motivate. Your personal experiences help shape some of your current thought processes. Regardless of whatever your personality type is, you can continue to be a dynamic leader without sacrificing the core essence of your being.

Becoming a dynamic leader excites and provides an energy that motivates your associates to achieve their desired goals and objectives. Think of the presidential primaries and the election process in general. The following that each candidate has speaks more to their ability to reach their base's emotional, mental, and social desires. Rarely, will you find a person who will align himself or herself with a candidate who does not speak to their core values and beliefs. The candidate's ability to present a personal power or aura among the base continues to motivate and align those with his or her overall vision and goals. The candidate's followers will take that energy and passion for rallying others to supporting their cause, or to reinforce the values of what the candidate is attempting to portray.

If you scour some of the more prominent magazines and newsworthy articles, you will notice the stories of leaders and their paths towards success. Each leader portrayed has a level of humility which I find as refreshing and essential as part of the Four Fits of Dynamic Leadership. Even though the associates will work for you because of their basic wants and needs, they may not truly embrace you if you do not have a sense of compassion or humility. This concept does not mean you need to have a bleeding heart and save the world, but the most dynamic leaders in the 21st century understand that their style of leadership is as essential as their managerial skills.

Thus, this is the concept of dynamic leadership in the 21st century for the context of this book. Management and leadership skills that were adequate decades ago may not be as useful today. In most settings, there needs to be a suitable union between leadership and management. Real leadership comes from within you. If you demonstrate leadership to your peers and your associates, you will likely run into less difficulty in reaching the organization's core objectives. Continuing to lead by leading from within yourself and utilizing the Four Fits will provide you more leverage and opportunities for your path towards success.

Each of these Fits provided throughout the book is a foundation. As you continue to read this book, I encourage you to not only think about the axioms presented in the book but to develop your Fits. Everybody is different, and out of respect for each difference, I could never imagine offering something that is inclusive of everyone's persona. As such, laying a foundation or blueprint design for your leadership style helps enhance who you currently are at this moment.

Consider the design of your dream home that the builder provides. You look at the layout and dimensions of that home; however, you feel that certain tweaks need to be made to fit your vision of home. As you continue through the building process, you make multiple selections as to cabinetry, type of flooring, and paint color.

The Four Fits of Dynamic Leadership is a simple blueprint where you decide what fits best for you. The Four Fits provides you an opportunity to continue to think outside the box consistently. You are permitted to return to the matrix or box design of the Four Fits or some other theoretical concept as your ability to combine abstract and linear thinking and consistently applying the concepts gives you a competitive advantage over others. You remove the shackles that bound others you know, or may have worked for, or even are currently working for today. By being dynamic, you eliminate the concept of groupthink.

Groupthink affects each set of people in their current environment. When you were a student working on the four-person project, you had a leader and followers. When your company broke you up into groups, you had a similar set up of a leader and followers. When the teams go into developing their project or assignment, some of the members continue to fall in line with whatever the group consensus is because it is safe and easy for them to do so. Accepting groupthink avoids the consequences and responsibility of your actions. Groupthink robs others of the ability to think for themselves.

Even though there are no hard numbers to prove this, I would estimate approximately 85% of people engage in a groupthink and follower mentality. This number could include some of the current leaders of your organization! Even though that individual thought is encouraged in some meetings and conferences, groupthink frequently takes over and changes the tone of the event.

For example, you are at a conference with industry professionals. Despite the likelihood that many of your peers are at or near the same title or level of responsibility, the conference and event feature the individuals who feel that their experience and expertise supersedes that of their peers. Although, this may not be their entire thought process; a particular dynamic occurs. The other members of the conference or event become more silent and not as engaged due to the excessive comments by several other members. This particular form of reluctance from the individuals results in diminishing any value or return of ongoing participation in feedback.

After the conference, you find yourself at an after-hours dinner or function with the same peers. What you often find is that you will obtain more information sharing and knowledge after the original agenda because the conversation is likely no longer dominated by the same individual. The potential for groupthink to occur dissipates, and the different personalities begin to shine.

I use this example of groupthink to enhance the concept of the Four Fits. Sometimes, you do not have to become the most noticed or vocal individual in the room. A quiet confidence can also hold your leadership, only to provide the appropriate opportunity to display your strengths in the most opportune of moments. A holistic development of your leadership style should include the ability to diagnose the environment, and become more aware of how you project your consciousness to your immediate surroundings.

Numerous individuals can define dynamic leadership in various ways. For the philosophical concepts of this book, dynamic leadership is a holistic process by dividing four processes, or the Four Fits, into ways that the individual incorporates his or her leadership style into a more complex and diverse workplace. The demands and expectations made with fewer resources have increased over the years, and are likely to continue to do so. Leaders must understand that simply managing core objectives, missions, and values of an organization is not viable if the organizational leaders refuse to understand, relate, lead, and empower his or her employees. Each of the Four Fits contains axioms, or beliefs, which accentuate each Fit. Even though it is possible for someone to develop additional axioms that fit best for that person or organization, I provide a relative basic foundation to build your Four Fits.

CHAPTER 2

THE MENTAL FIT

IF YOU HAVE not read the *Four Fits of Holistic Growth* and are not familiar with the Four Fits concept, I believe it is necessary to establish a foundation (Duncan, 2016). The Four Fits is a process that you go through in developing a deeper understanding of your internal and external environment. As you become more versed in your understanding and use of the Four Fits, the dimensions inside each Fit grow. Your growth within this holistic model enables you to blend different aspects of each fit to improve and expand the spherical model as illustrated in Table 1.

Growth within each Fit should be at a pace that is best for you. Your feelings and thought processes affect your style of learning. If you are an emphatic learner, you possess a capacity to learn at a different rate than those who are more analytical and linear in thought processes. A link exists between distributed and collaborative learning, which draws from empathy, and critical thinking skills. Research shows that those who demonstrate the capacity for empathy and the ability to be non-judgmental tend to increase their ability to improve their capacity to learn and interact with others. Cognitive benefits exist when empathy is present in a learner which include: insight into different perspectives, discouraging superficial problem examination, discouraging belief rigidity, and an analysis of flexibility (Briggs, 2014).

Even if you are not an empathetic individual or learner, you are still able to cultivate your thought process in a fashion necessary to connect with those who follow your lead. I am not imploring you to cry in meetings; however, developing a non-linear method frame of thinking will help you develop the ability to create a bridge between your associates and yourself. Numerous leadership books and training models exist that focuses on emphatic learning even though that is not the stated intent of the book. If you have read such books, there is an emotional or empathetic connection you are learning which has likely helped your style of leadership and management.

The Mental Fit is an expansion of the above discussion. To become a more dynamic leader, creating a balanced mental mindset is essential. If you are already in a leadership role, you likely have some form of mental resiliency in addressing some of the stressful events that occurred in your career. As you become more entrenched in your position, you are more jaded and develop a "been there, done that" mentality. I recall a situation where I spoke to an administrator about an associate who had disciplinary issues. The administrator was in the industry in various roles for approximately 15+ years. Despite the situation at hand, the administrator appeared jaded about the matter. Without probing further, I am relatively confident that being in the position for such a long time with an emphasis towards reporting and other statistical metrics created the "been there, done that" mentality.

I am not advocating that every supervisor, manager, or executive should put on a cape and shield to fight all the world's perils. Mentally, this individual may have reached the proverbial wall and focused on one crucial matter: survival. With a stronger push towards analytics, there is a shift from emphatic learning and leading to keeping the statistics relevant. As someone who has been through numerous course and exercises emphasizing statistical modeling, one thing the statistics and metrics do not show is what the numbers represent. Understanding the story beyond the statistics is a critical component of emphatic learning under the Mental Fit.

The numbers do lie sometimes. The lie may not exist in the figures regarding forecasting and budgeting; however, there are intangible factors that affect the statistics in ways that the designed categories do not show. When creating a spreadsheet for your report, you look for key measurables; however, the question you ask the next time you look at your operations scorecard is in what areas are the intangible factors addressed?

I will address this from an auditing standpoint. When conducting an audit, there are numerous scoring criteria or metrics used to determine if compliance exists relating to the company's best practices or the industry's performance standards at a facility or building. After conducting the audit, an exit interview should take place between the auditor and the facility leadership. When going over the audit scores, it is easy to demonstrate scoring on what is right and what is wrong. This type of thinking is an example of non-emphatic thinking and analysis.

The reliance on the numbers within the scoring criteria is black and white. However, the facility or location you audited may have certain dynamic factors in play that the scores do not reflect. Turnover, new leadership, staffing challenges, and lack of communication could be reasons why the scores may not be as high as leadership preferred. Other factors could be in play that neither the auditor nor the immediate leadership are aware of before the auditing process.

Emphatic leadership and learning benefit the auditing process. Listening to leadership needs and issues may create avenues for ongoing education and development. Being capable of assessing the facility beyond the numbers may create an opportunity to improve not only the audit scores but also provide an opportunity to align best practices along with the facility's challenges. The buy-in provided by emphatic leadership to the other party creates an ongoing dialogue between the parties that results in improved scores in the next audit and more alignment with organizational goals and best practices.

Emphatic leadership helps identify the strengths and challenges of your associates. As a leader or manager of a facility or organization, you may be in tune with the requirements of your average day to day operations; however, your associates may not understand the reasoning and rationale between some of the policies that are in place. Many people may surround you who have a mentality that something is not their job. Even if surrounded by energy leeches, you still possess the ability to motivate, lead, and influence those who have that mentality to buy-in to your stated and desired goals.

Possessing the inherent traits of understanding what proverbial buttons to push provides value to your team by understanding the challenges of your staff. Believe it or not, that individual who continuously believes that something is not his or her job is a leader in disguise, because that individual often does not prescribe to groupthink. I know this may sound irrational because not everyone provides fit to an organization; however, understanding this person may provide significant value to your team.

Even though no system, person, or process is perfect, that does not mean that you should stop striving to achieve perfection. The Mental Fit is a process that asks you to continuously seek perfection in a manner where you are able to monitor, evaluate, and reflect. Leadership is an ongoing learning process. Despite the material that you will find throughout this book, the concepts of the Four Fits will continue to evolve to challenge you to seek perfection as close you can. Possessing the ability to adjust, adapt, and grow despite your successes will continue to set you apart as a dynamic leader with a willingness to embrace the constant change you encounter.

The Mental Fit, along with each other Fit, contains several axioms that help accentuate the individual Fit concept. As stated before, over time, you are free to develop your axioms or incorporate scenarios where you decide which Fit matches with the appropriate decision-making. This book is not to quantify your leadership abilities or skills but to expand the consciousness that already exists within your mind.

AXIOM #1: SLOW DOWN THE TONE, PACE, AND TEMPO OF YOUR ENVIRONMENT

I am a huge fan of sports and often draw up sports strategy and analogies when it comes to leadership techniques and management styles. Some of the more accomplished leadership books originate from the great coaches of the game from John Wooden, Vince Lombardi, and Phil Jackson among others. Even though sports have different objectives and goals in mind, it is up to management and coaching to work together to bring the right pieces to make things work. Some of the phrases you hear are somewhat cliché but stable in reasoning.

One of the most often used clichés I created for myself and use personally is that you must slow down the tone, pace, and tempo of your environment. Imagine being in an emergency situation where you must respond quickly or lives could be significantly affected. In this situation, you have the distinct responses of fight or flight. I believe if you take it one step further, those who responded to that particular emergency situation displayed a level head and exercised calm. The calm projected spreads to others around that individual and creates clarity. That moment of clarity helps others respond effectively in the emergency situation with minimal impact to those affected.

Even though all situations are not considered life or death, demonstrating an ability to slow everything down in your mind is a strong leadership trait. One thing you must never forget is that if you are in a leadership role, someone is always watching you. When a crisis develops no matter how small or large, you must develop an ability to mentally take a few steps back and take control of the situation.

Throughout my professional career, I have seen numerous cases where those in a leadership position show cracks in the façade when encountering a high leverage situation. Even if the external world around them becomes out of sync, they become lost in the current that ebbs and flows around them. Once you become sucked into the current, it is hard to regain form. As a result, decisions are made in haste or without the foresight of what the consequences may be from their decision-making.

When I think of slowing down the tone, pace, and tempo of my environment, I think of standing in the middle of chaos swirling around. The debris depicts the chaos personified by the situation. I stand in the midst of the tempest of this storm trying to see what is around me, as well as what is outside of me. I cannot see what is around the debris.

From the strength of my mind and positive energy, I attempt to move the debris around until there is clarity in front of me.

As we continue to subject ourselves to a variety of information, our mind is unknowingly sped up to the pace where it can be difficult to process and assimilate what is happening. Instead, we are forced to encounter some of our primal thoughts and emotions, sometimes without being able to clearly absorb and understand what it is that we face.

Being in a leadership role is not too much different. More information is available through a variety of means and input, and we are sometimes asked to make decisions very quickly. Once you allow yourself to be sped up by the information, you unravel and lose focus as to what may be the best decision based on the circumstances. How often have you been faced with a decision that needed to be acted on quickly, when the pressure is intense? The wrong decisions, words, or actions you take may have profound implications on the situation. As a result, the desired outcome of the situation, or your day in general, is thrown astray. From there, you are left picking up the pieces or trying to recover from that scenario.

You do not have to be a control freak or OCD to be in control. The concept of being in control involves your ability to ensure that you have created balance in your environment. Creating an equilibrium provides you the opportunity to assess the current landscape, and make the appropriate strategic decisions. When you do not have balance or equilibrium established, you fail to see the entire picture.

Think of developing your equilibrium and vision in leadership as driving a vehicle either on a straight, flat road compared to a hilly, curvy road. Vision is necessary for administration to see what influences exist around you and your associates. Your vision should be able to see most events within a 360-degree arc, and within control. Your equilibrium in leadership involves balance and restraint. The ability to remain steady and calm under duress is an essential trait of a dynamic leader.

Demonstrating how to bring your organization within center as a leader provides clarity and a compass to your associates.

Driving on a straight, flat road allows you to have great vision as to what is before you, around you, and behind you. If anything goes astray in either of these directions, you have the presence of mind to make the necessary adjustments on the road. You are essentially permitted the maximum amount of time to determine if you need to overcorrect to avoid an accident, avoid debris, or any other obstacles that may come in your path.

Driving on a hilly or curvy terrain does not afford you the same luxury. When you are driving with your visibility affected, you must remain sharp and focused. Otherwise, you may not be able to react as you could on a straight, flat road. If something zoomed over the horizon, you must quickly make a decision. You quickly must decide what to do at that given moment. If you do not panic and keep your wits about you, you make the appropriate decision and continue driving until the road straightens out the flat and narrow terrain again.

In leadership, similar to life, the road will continue to be hilly and curvy. Often, you will not have the opportunity to be on a straight and flat road with great vision around. Keeping a level head despite the uncertainty of the terrain around you is essential in being a dynamic leader. Establishing your mental resolve despite the complex situations that confront you is not an easy task. However, being a dynamic leader is not an easy task as well.

Slowing down the tone, pace, and tempo should not only be a mindset, but it should also be an ideology. Demonstrating the ability to do so shows your peers you are effectively in control of not only the situation but shows command of yourself as a leader and motivator. If you seek and desire to be in a leadership role, or if you are attempting to enhance your visibility as a leader, you must remember that someone is always watching you. Someone is looking up to you whether you know it or not. We will discuss this more under the Personal Power Fit; however, you must understand that even those who recently joined the organization may be observing you and your actions.

Setting the tone is similar to communicating your expectations and vision to your associates. As an administrator of a skilled nursing facility, you understand that ultimately the purpose of the facility is to provide care to the residents. However, if the actions are not correlating with this knowledge, a disconnect forms. The disconnection of your tone sends conflicting messages to your associates and undermines the desired goals of achieving quality care for the residents. Chaos and uncertainty develop, and the intended message and objectives often change as you devote an enormous amount of energy attempting to re-calibrate the tone.

The pace of your organization and leadership style is an ebb and flow. Despite the type of organization or industry you are in, it is critical to understand that highs and lows are part of the business cycle. As a dynamic leader, you set the pace of how you are going to lead into each wave within the ebb and flow. Even if you are not familiar with surfing, imagine being on a surfboard, and you need to make an adjustment with the waves oncoming. If you keep going at the same pace and pitch, you will wipeout. However, if you adjust accordingly before hitting the waves, you compensate and demonstrate the capability of riding the wave.

Your leadership style should mirror that of surfing because you will have some turbulent times, and some golden times. Your ability to set the pace to keep your associates and organization in the balance creates stability and effectiveness to achieve desired outcomes. Often, the changes that occur are neither predictable nor identical. Steadying the pace in between the highs and lows show restraint and calm to those who follow your lead.

Controlling the tempo of your environment is a strong leadership trait. Effectiveness derives from the defined pace of your environment and organization determined by creating the appropriate measure of how you will achieve your core objectives. For an organization that may be struggling in customer service satisfaction scores, leadership should explore in what areas they are struggling the most and develop the appropriate training that fits the associates responsible for customer service. Rather than extolling the mission and values of the organization, it would be more appropriate to start over with the fundamentals of customer service. The associates may also find it beneficial to have a forum where they can openly discuss the challenges they encounter while attempting to achieve a high level of customer service.

At the conclusion of each axiom is a worksheet that underscores some of the common themes found throughout the axiom. Similar to the *Four Fits of Holistic Growth*, the worksheets are designed to help you, as the reader, relate your personal situations and scenarios to the axiom itself (Duncan, 2016). We work in different industries, fields, and work with a different set of rules; however, the basic foundation of dynamic leadership is the same and is universally applied. The worksheets also provide a forum for you to go back and review what you wrote down, and presents an opportunity to be used again.

The first worksheet covers how do you set the tone, pace, and tempo as a leader. When completing the worksheet, please keep in mind that the effectiveness of these worksheets throughout the book starts with becoming honest with yourself. You must demonstrate the ability to be able to do the proverbial look at yourself in the mirror in understanding certain situations and circumstances that you encounter within your role as a leader. There is no right or wrong answer in completing these answers, so your honesty and openness will help you develop into a holistic and dynamic leader.

The purpose of Worksheet #1 is to examine or discuss a situation where you apply the tone, pace, and tempo axiom. You can use a situation that happened to you directly or a situation you observed where you might provide a different outlook. The results of the exercise vary depending on the level of experience you currently have. If you are a more experienced manager, I challenge you to think of a situation that personally affected you, and a situation that may have affected someone else you know, or a story you heard at a networking event.

I coached an administrator one day who was relatively new to her position. She informed me that she took over an operation that recently dismissed the previous administrator. As she was fairly young and the building had experienced high turnover, she felt the many challenges as overwhelming. We discussed the dynamics of her operation, from her background and the location of this building in a rural area.

I informed her that no matter if she had much experience or was relatively new, the larger issue was the dynamics of the building. Operations in rural communities do not embrace change as quickly as more developed and urban areas. Although turnover happens everywhere, a sense of familiarity and stability occurred which was no fault of her own. I informed her that to make the change fluid and efficient; I encouraged her to consider the tone, pace, and tempo axiom under the Mental Fit.

I recommended that she incorporate a plan and set a date in intervals to assess the changes and to implement her vision. I informed her that although she must continue to reach organizational objectives, she should continue to evaluate her relationship with her staff at different intervals. Assessing the strategic and leadership vision in 30 days will provide a landscape for her to be aware of what obstacles are present. I recommended that she phase her leadership changes during months two and four, with an overall personal assessment of herself along with her staff in six months.

When completing this worksheet, think of this story above and relate the process of change to your leadership style. Change is a dynamic that is unpredictable to staff and the organization, as numerous variables exist. Understanding what the variables are, and learning how to incorporate them into your leadership strategy effectively sets the pace for how you provide continuity and clarity.

As you complete each worksheet, I remind you that it is okay to create as many scenarios as possible. As stated before, there is no correct answer to the situation. If you polled 50 people to come up with a solution to an obstacle encountered, you might come up 50 different answers. In solving complex issues as a dynamic leader, there is no multiple choice, nor answer key. You develop and cultivate your leadership style to the best of your ability.

AXIOM #2: UNDERSTANDING THE 3 C'S: CLARITY, COMMUNICATION, AND COMMITMENT

The second axiom under the Mental Fit involves the three C's: clarity, commitment, and communication. This axiom does not necessarily have to be exclusive to leadership, as it is also applicable to interpersonal relationships you may have with your significant other, or extensive interactions with others. The three C's is part of the business model of my consulting company, J.I. Enterprises. To establish a stable relationship with my clients, I keep the three C's in mind from start to finish. By building the three C's, a rapport exists between the customer and myself where expectations are understood implicitly and explicitly.

Change is inevitable in every industry and its operations. We never know what to expect from the moment we wake up to the time that we leave for the day. The days are full of highs and lows, and challenges toward your mental sanity exist. Despite the challenges you encounter in leadership with change, think about how it affects your staff.

Some associates struggle with change. Notwithstanding those in charge being hardwired to address changes, the psychological impact of changes in the workplace may differ from associate to associate. Some may embrace the changes; while some may "shut down" or regress in their work performance. When a change occurs, the question you must ask yourself is how, as a leader, will you be able to communicate or address the changes that happen in the workplace?

A dynamic leader must understand the value of clarity not only in an organizational setting but also from a personal standpoint. You are not able to execute changes from senior leadership appropriately if you are not certain as to why the changes are necessary. If procedural changes came from your industry regulations, poor understanding as to what the changes are could produce mixed results or complications in your organization.

Without clarity, you will have organizational chaos. The intended message becomes distorted, and a lack of fluidity in your leadership styles and organizational performances by your associates occurs. No matter how many associates you are responsible for under your guidance, lack of clarity creates confusion and frustration amongst your associates and apparent frustration in yourself.

Lack of transparency creates conflict in leadership. Lack of clarity also lowers the likelihood of innovation. A 2003 study examining the relationship between clarity and leadership revealed a correlation with a lack of clarity and leadership regarding defining clear organizational objectives (West et al., 2003). The more clarity leadership provides, the likelihood of embracing and encouraging effective participation by associates increase.

To establish transparency as a dynamic leader, you must begin understanding the personal and professional goals of your staff. To understand clarity, you develop a sense of purpose. Therefore, you must seek to understand the reasons why your associates are working under your leadership. Figure out what is their personal or professional motivation to come into work every day. Although you will have some associates who are there to collect a check, you will be surprised how often your associates are looking to you for direction.

Providing clarity to your associates will help them buy into your leadership style. Taking the time to understand that your staff members are significant shareholders into your leadership mantra gives them value, a sense of belonging, and purpose. Even though the majority of us will be required to work until at least retirement age, our goals as influential leaders are to provide these tools to increase organizational effectiveness.

Remember, we live in an era of self-gratification, self-empowerment, and selfies. Social media provides many of us an opportunity to show the world how "relevant" we are. This particular frame of thinking carries over to the workplace resulting in potential conflict. The evolution of the workplace is another dynamic factor of change as benefits, wages, and the number of tenured employees changed over the years. As such, your interpersonal skills, or clarity, are more important than ever.

Understanding the changes in your world outside of the workplace is as critical as understanding the changes in your world from within the workplace. Thus, creating a structure within your organization and leadership style that mirrors that of your external environment will assist you in aligning your leadership and organizational goals along with your associates' personal and professional goals.

Commitment is the second of the three C's. Commitment comes from your ability to connect to the vision, goals, and objectives of an organization. Commitment also comes from your capacity to connect with your associates in a manner that aligns them with your leadership style and vision. Commitment is valuable in building relationships with your stakeholders, internal and external, to your organization and industry.

Commitment shows a lot about you as a dynamic leader. Often, we find ourselves discussing matters and making promises, and guarantees, without thoroughly thinking through the results of your words and lack of action. Imagine that you are in a meeting with several managers discussing a new project. During this project that needs implementation, committees require a determination regarding resource allocation towards the overall project. Because you are relatively new to the management team, you blindly volunteer your team or yourself to commit to the project without fully understanding all that the project entails.

A fundamental lack of understanding creates a problem for you and your team because the project requires more time and labor hours than what you have allocated within your labor forecast. The unit or facility that you are responsible for has their challenges that seriously need attention. Without fully understanding the indirect effects of your commitment, you have ignored some of the areas where your attention is truly needed.

Unfortunately, this happens a lot. One of the biggest challenges of leadership is restraint and patience. Sometimes we are so wired to be successful or the first to accomplish something, that we lose track of the big picture. Sometimes the big picture is not about the recognition on a larger scale. Instead, the big picture can be what is going on in your "house." You cannot try to blaze another trail to add a feather to your cap if you are not willing to address the mundane, but legitimate concerns that are plaguing your day to day activities.

Consistency could be a subset of commitment. Sometimes it is not so much the words that we utter around our team rather than the consistent nature of how we express ourselves as leaders. The message that you are trying to get across to your associates will become distorted if you lack the ability to be even-keeled during the highs and lows. All too often, we see those in management roles bring inconsistent energy to the workplace. If this energy carries from within, the body language and perceptions of you as a leader are unbalanced and uncertain.

I recall working a manager who was not a strong leader. I say this because you actually could not tell which way she was coming or going. I remember when I asked for guidance or clarification of something in general, the responses and body language were determinant as to her overall mode of thinking. Other co-workers had similar difficulties in approaching this manager, as well as losing confidence in her ability to lead.

Consistency provides stability in an organization. Consistency establishes and maintains your reputation with your staff and peers. Accountability is significantly affected by your level of uniformity. Recall a situation where you have a senior member of leadership who was not consistent in his or her behavior, and the expectations were uncertain. As a dynamic leader, you maintain a culture of calm when practicing consistency.

Morale is affected by poor consistency displayed by a leader. Uncertainty breeds contempt, which could negatively influence the performance of your team. As a leader, if you are not able to become consistent in your mannerisms or addressing a situation, the more disruptive associates may take advantage of the discord, and develop a more negative subculture from within.

Consistency in leadership comes from two different methods: internal and external. Internally, consistency comes from inside you. As a dynamic leader, you must ask yourself are you consistent with your methods of communication and leading? Do you have a significant variance between how you are away from work and when you are at the office? If you exhibit an entirely different personality away from work than you do at work, the message that you are likely extending to your associates is unbalanced.

As stated before, consistency is also external. The external manner of your consistency could derive from your administration of the policies and procedures that are in place. Your ability to effectively deal with human resource matters come from whether or not you are willing not to look at the bigger picture. A dynamic leader has a strong personality and is decisive in his or her decision-making. In our current litigious society, inconsistent handling or failure to follow the set rules and policies create a systems breakdown, and possibly affect employee morale.

Communication is the final element of the three C's. Communication is how we exchange information with others verbally and nonverbally. Another dimension to add for the sake of discussion under dynamic leadership is electronic communication. Despite the knowledge of the effects of effective communication, issues still exist that continue to affect the complex nature of our relationships with others. This remains true whether it is our leadership among teams, or amongst other leaders.

The art of communication is similar to the entire Four Fits process in that communication is not linear, it is circular. Communication exists in a circular loop where the source and receiver frequently change position once the message has been transmitted, and when the message has been received (Hackman & Johnson, 2013). As communication is circular in nature, it can also be viewed as an infinite loop until communication ceases. Understanding the relationship between the two parties is beneficial for leaders to develop effective methods of communicating with their team.

Even though we all learned about communication from high school and college courses, communication is one of the primary reasons why misunderstandings occur, if one party is not in tune with the other. Communication is critical in determining whether or not others will buy into your message, intent, and, purpose.

Think about how you are a part of a planning committee. The purpose of the planning committee is to come up with new employee retention programs and activities to show appreciation for all the work that they do. You set a designated date to have a small event recognizing the efforts and commitment to the organization. You are the nominated person for securing the event space where the appreciation party is to take place after hours.

Because you have a lot on your plate with other projects and activities, you continue to delay reaching out to the facility. The Committee meets at regular intervals within a 30-day window to discuss any new updates, and you continue to state that everything is secure. Less than a week before the event, you attempt to call, and space is not available. You frantically try calling other areas within a reasonable distance, only to find out that other venues are booked as well.

Unfortunately, this event happens more often than not when it comes to communication. Vague communication could have been easily avoidable if you notified the committee that time was a constraint that affected your ability to secure the event space. Advising the committee could have created a reassignment of team duties which could increase the likelihood of the party being a success.

When working with different people who have different personalities, communication is vital to ensure that everyone is on the same page, moving towards the same goal. Being a dynamic leader requires you to understand the strengths and challenges of your teammates and associates to ensure that the message is well-received and understood.

Communication is relevant when it comes to electronic communication, whether it is a direct messaging platform, email, or text messages. Technology creates an increased speed of delivering messages; however, this also increases the likelihood of the message being misunderstood or taken out of context. What you type and send leaves a more lasting impression versus verbal communication. Despite the use of any form of electronic communication, I recommend that you review your messages to ensure that the message is clear, concise, and capable of ensuring that the reader can clearly read and understand the purpose and intent of the message.

The only caveat about this type of communication is that, as you may recall the circuitous loop between the sender and receiver, the receiver must be willing to review, comprehend, and understand the content of the message provided. If you are in charge of a team which must act on the information given, you cannot make the assumption that each individual will understand the contents of the message. As such, you must be willing to adjust the content or the tone of the message to fit the receiver of the message.

I recall an audit I conducted for two clients in a similar time span. Before the audit, numerous emails were sent indicating what to anticipate for the audit and to provide the tools necessary to score well. Both clients received follow-up emails, and I provided them the opportunity for additional training, as well as promoting my accessibility. One of the clients took advantage of that opportunity; the other client did not. The result was a 40% difference in scores between the two clients.

The same information was made available at the same time. The client who did not perform not only had communication issues, but had a breakdown of internal systems. After conducting the exit interview, there was a lot of finger-pointing and blame among the team, as well as blame placed on me. After hearing their concerns, I pointed out several observations.

I noted that ownership had to occur from within yourself. Accountability is not something a leader alone can provide; it is something that has to come from that individual team. As a dynamic leader, you can provide all the tools and resources available; however, what I realized was the importance of working on team buy-in. Exhibiting patience and maintaining a calm demeanor, I continued to explain the necessity of the audit and to underscore that it is a team effort. I continued to work with the team to the point where ownership and accountability kicked in over time. By the next audit the client's score had gone up more than 35 points.

Communication involves criticism as much as it includes praise. Similar to discussing commitment, consistency is the measure you must seek when handling both. Obviously, it is easier to effuse praise compared to being critical; however, criticism creates growth. We are acutely aware that no one is perfect, but that should not prevent us from striving towards perfection together.

Criticism is difficult because the sender and the receiver have different levels of understanding. As a leader or manager, you have leverage over the other individual because you are communicating the challenges he or she has. Try as hard as possible to avoid using the concepts of right and wrong. The word "wrong" stings and can cause the intended message to be misconstrued from the start. Enacting a dialogue as an attempt to promote some form of equal footing in the conversation assists you in delivering the message needed.

Constructive criticism is difficult if you are not intuitive to the other party's non-verbal cues, or if your non-verbal cues are not presentable. As you may previously recall, your ability to be intuitive to your associates assist you in communication and encourages team buy-in. This particular logic applies to constructive criticism as well. Everyone is working for some reason, which mainly is to provide financial support for individual needs. As such, understanding the real value of your associates, you can lead them better if you keep them engaged and motivated.

Even if there is an opportunity for improvement, ensure that the associate is aware of the purpose of the meeting. Give him or her the opportunity to speak openly about the situation. Doing so is critical because allowing them to vent or express themselves help relieve or diffuse some of the inherent tension of the meeting or inside the individual. Allowing the associate to speak also helps you determine how to proceed in engaging the associate for the educational opportunity. You may have had a "game plan" as to how you desired to approach the subject; however, certain non-verbal clues may exist that lead you to believe that you may need to change your approach based on the situation.

Unfortunately, with criticism, comes confrontation. No one wants to feel or perceive that they are wrong. We all try to put our best foot forward but sometimes, we get in our way, which is life. When engaging the associate, recap what happened with the facts only. Sticking to the facts and removing emotions from your conversation provides you a stronger likelihood to communicate more efficiently.

If there is a coachable moment, offer alternatives to the associate. If this situation applies, I often recommend giving the associate the opportunity to provide alternatives first. Providing options continue an open dialogue and sometimes a brief conversation makes the associate acutely aware that there are other ways to address that situation or process. Remember, your objective is to be of assistance and not a detriment to your associate's overall performance.

After you both have an opportunity to discuss the situation, recommendations, and necessary education, promote an ongoing open dialogue. Even though the associate still may not be accepting of his or her situation, you should continue to keep the lines of communication open. Sometimes, it even may be necessary to check on the associate over the next several days or week to strengthen or rebuild the rapport to ensure that the message was accepted and understood by the associate.

To conduct business and for people to understand your viewpoint, you should know how the other person is thinking. By doing so, you are temporarily setting aside your thought process to incorporate their ideas to get your desired objectives. Communicating in a manner or language that is clear and concise to the intended party articulates the message more clearly.

A strong relationship exists between effective communication and strong leadership. Communication competence is an essential tool for effective leadership (Flauto, 1999). Your ability to choose a behavior for your communication that is appropriate for the tone, pace, and tempo of your environment increases the likelihood of receiving the message.

The worksheet for this axiom features how you relate to the three C's. Within Worksheet #2, each exercise within provides you an opportunity exploring and identifying your use of the three C's: clarity, commitment, and communication. Think of how it affects your leadership style and your personality. We all have encountered scenarios where we look back and wish that we had handled it a little differently.

Research is always a good way to enhance what you are learning throughout the book. If you have a strong grasp of other leadership and management theory principles, I encourage you to implement them for this worksheet. Is there a particular theorem or principle that could have applied in these worksheets? Remember that the purpose of the Four Fits of Dynamic Leadership is to build a foundation; however, you can craft your own version or add additional axioms for your personal Four Fits. Therefore, finding examples or open discussions with other leaders is beneficial. I say this because there is a wealth of knowledge available, and there is nothing wrong with acquiring more to make yourself an effective and dynamic leader.

Axiom #3: Learn How to Adjust, Adapt, and Move Forward

In the first two axioms under the Mental Fit, I am confident that you are seeing a certain theme developing. The theme developed throughout this first Fit is the concept of maintaining control. As a dynamic leader, you must exhibit control of your faculties to motivate, lead, and inspire others to walk the path you are willing to show them. Developing and maintaining control is a delicate balance to keep so you can achieve your key objectives and goals.

Take into consideration that control should not be associated with the context of ownership or property. We must continue to value and appreciate our team because, without the collective efforts of the team, greatness cannot be accomplished. I recall a phrase that I used and still believe to this day when motivating my team which was, "I cannot be great unless you are great. For that to happen, we have to be great together." That statement still has value to me to this day which is discussed in more detail under the Emotional Fit.

The last axiom under the Mental Fit involves your ability to adapt to your internal and external environments. In our current roles, we encounter endless analytics. Analytics provide insight into operational, financial, and strategic progress. Comparisons between different periods are used to determine if the organization is progressing in a manner that is consistent with overall growth, or to limit financial losses. We mine these numbers to identify trends and make the necessary adjustments.

For those who have completed their secondary education degrees or management classes, we encounter numerous managerial courses that focus on financial figures, learning how to manage a balance sheet, or understand statistical modeling. A vast amount of information exists through various intermediaries that help expand our foundation of knowledge. Despite all these courses and training sessions, understanding the intangibles is often not addressed.

Change is a process that occurs virtually in every entity, individual, and life. Change is a process that is unpredictable and an unknown. Some people are more capable of accepting or managing change than others. If you are reading this, you are likely in a role where you have been able to accommodate and embrace change to some degree. Otherwise, you would not be as compelled to read a book of this nature if you were willing to accept complacency.

Change affects people in different ways. This statement holds especially true in organizational cultures. Several reasons exist why people are resistant to change in the workplace: lacking the competency to change; the feeling of being overloaded and overwhelmed; healthy skepticism; and fear that change threatens their notions of themselves (Schuler, 2003). Although there are other reasons why resistance to change occurs, we can focus on these four examples.

Diagnosing the resistance to change and developing a solid plan to address the resistance provide the organization an opportunity to understand their new roles or the duties required of them. The classic response when adding more tasks is how much compensation will they get in return. Often, there is not a raise or financial incentive tied to the change, so your ability to communicate how the change benefits them may help take the sting away from not providing a financial incentive.

I do stress; however, that you do not discuss the financial status of the organization. Examining the financial ability to compensate the change could be a detriment in a way that you could lose high-performing teammates. Those who are the most resistant to change will most likely stay on board regardless of the changes that occur. However, the associates who may be ambitious or willing to take their talents elsewhere begin to lose an incentive to stay motivated and think of long term employment elsewhere. One thing to never lose track of is that as competitive as your industry is concerning stakeholders, your organizational competition comes from their ability to attract your more talented performers because you applied an across the board "we have no money" mentality.

Resistance to change is a natural reaction for those who are affected by the change process itself. Logic and rationality are traits not often associated with resistance to change. The resistance to change is more of an emotional, instinctive response wherein the mind assumes the worse. Several reasons could explain why such resistance exists: instability, media sources, friends/family, and fear of the unknown.

Something that leaders may not take into consideration is that the majority of people within the organizational culture heavily encounter negativity, especially in the media. This statement is not to assail the media industry; however, the negative images of recession, layoffs, people losing mortgages, plant shutdowns dominate the headlines more than the positive highlights. Even though it is debatable that the media conjures up images of fear and worry, it is not easy to brush aside the constant barrage of the subjected imagery that people encounter. Social media, depending on the industry or tenor of the conversation, can also provide an adverse effect on employees when times are down.

The organizational culture is also a shared culture. Diversity in the workplace has increased dramatically over the years. Coworkers now consist of people who are different regarding race, sex, religion, transgender/sexual orientation, and other prevalent attitudes and personalities seen throughout our external environment. With that said, this is an additional element to consider when factoring change. The majority of workers in the organizational culture have different reasons for motivation and company loyalty. Therefore, it is incumbent upon leaders to be responsive and intuitive to the psychological make-up of their employees to help mitigate the change process.

For example, a health care provider is responsible for implementing government mandated electronic medical records to reduce documentation, medical, and prescription errors. Research showed that a reduction in medical errors could reasonably improve overall health-care outcomes for patients, and increase efficiencies in work processes (Patel et al., 2012). For those responsible for implementing the change, resistance is evident due to perceived bias or a low comfort level of performing the necessary work processes in their customary fashion.

During the adoption and implementation process, the lack of energy or willingness to embrace change results in additional errors in the conversion process, costing the provider numerous man-hours and other indirect financial costs. Even though any new technology or innovation may have its share of bugs and hiccups, a negative mindset towards the change slows down the intended effects of the change initiative.

As a member of senior leadership, you are responsible for implementing a new work process where the intended goal is to provide more operational efficiencies, cut down on redundant or duplicate processes, and free up your associates to perform other ancillary functions of their primary position. The proposed process is a dynamic change where you anticipate resistance to change which could negatively affect morale. You discuss this with other managers to address how you can implement this process, as well as reassure staff that this is an improvement that benefits everyone.

If you decide to barrel headfirst into the process, you will likely encounter significant resistance. As influential leaders, a rule that you should be willing to accept and understand is that everyone working under you will not exhibit dynamic traits. Without a need to identifying the types of those who rally the troops towards negativity, an active leader should be aware that resistance to change is virtually inevitable. For most who are currently working under your care, or if you are leading a committee on a volunteer basis, you should recognize another truth: Everyone does not have the same energy, motivation, or passion as you do.

Recall a significant accomplishment you had in your life. It could be a promotion, graduation, or a hobby that took time to learn. Once this milestone is achieved, there is a level of elation that you experience, which you should have because you earned it. When you are sharing the news, especially with those who are not your closest of friends, family, or confidants, you will get a genuine "good for you" response. However, when you ask them to attend your graduation, buy your book, see your music performance, the turnout is lower than what you had wished.

Even though these significant life events create highs and lows of emotions, this also happens in the workplace. Your passion and energy for whatever you set out to accomplish do not necessarily mean that others will completely buy-in to your vision, especially when you are implementing a new process or environment in the workplace. The team may hear what the change is, but may not necessarily embrace it with the same level of interest as you do. The question to ask as a dynamic leader is, "How do you wind up communicating these changes, and rallying those around you to support this innovation?"

Let us return to the two examples regarding psychological barriers to change. Barriers to change may produce an environment of uncertainty, confusion, and unsettled emotions. Your organizational environment changed from a smooth, free-flowing operation to one of disruption and uncertainty. At this particular juncture of innovative change, you should demonstrate an ability to adjust and adapt to the new change of environment. Responding to change swiftly and efficiently to the alteration of your team's environment depends on your ability to improve individual leadership qualities from within. Therefore, in addressing these two situations, we will utilize the other axioms in combination with this axiom to solve these challenges.

What makes the Mental Fit dynamic is that you are taking this axiom, and combining it with the previous two axioms in addressing innovative changes. As a leader, you are consciously aware of who are the dissenters of change, those accepting of any change, or those who need guidance and clarification. Concerning the dissenters of change, the ones who likely could affect morale or demonstrate an intangible wall of resistance in general, you will need to rely on your ability to slow down the tone, pace, and tempo of this new environment.

Negativity is contagious and can quickly spread like wildfire if left unchecked. From lunch breaks, happy hours, social media, or text messages, those who exhibit a negative attitude slowly influences others to the point that more people slowly jump on the negativity train to nowhere. In circumstances such as these, you will need to adjust the tone of your message to ensure that the message is received favorably by the dissenters. Although you would like to achieve 100% buy-in from other individuals, addressing and allaying their concerns may reduce some of the negativity with more information.

When it comes to those who regularly display a negative mentality such as "That is not my job," or "I am only doing my job until it is time to go," you have to give them an avenue to vent, but allow them to vent through you. Often, these individuals just need to hear their point of views, even though it may not necessarily matter to them; however, it is better that you hear this rather than having it spread throughout the floor. This method may not necessarily dispel the negative energy entirely, but at the very least, there is communication and dialogue.

Utilizing the second axiom concerning the three C's provides you the opportunity to get your message across to all parties. Even though you cannot divulge the confidential or proprietary details involving the change, your demonstrated ability to be consistent under all conditions is to your benefit. Establish that you are an upbeat leader who rarely shows that internal or external pressures can rattle you. A common theme I observed over the years is that the managers who are rolling out the changes and display negative energy (i.e. stressed, short, or evasive) do more harm than good when rolling out the program.

How consistent is your message? As a dynamic leader, your goal is to try and slowly message the change into the folds of their minds. You do not have to obsess over the topic repeatedly; however, a continuous message of the upcoming changes takes away some of the shock value rather than a brief mention, and then the change without warning, which creates more chaos in the environment. Providing clarity to your team and clearly communicating the nature of these changes show that you are very much in control, attentive to the needs and concerns of your team and that you show a willingness to work with them throughout this entire process.

One of my clients had a high rate of turnover in critical positions, which is not uncommon for this particular industry. When the change occurred, it appeared it conveniently happened in the midst of a project or training for a process with the assumption that everyone was aware of the necessary foundation. When a new person joined the team, a natural trepidation existed. This individual was hired to perform all of these functions and now is expected to learn a new dynamic. I can guarantee you that each time someone received a similar message, it was not well received.

One source of the problem was that the expectations of this position involved poor communication to these individuals. When an event occurred where communication between that person and myself occurred, frustration existed because no one explicitly said, you are handling this as part of your normal, routine activities. Therefore, resistance was natural whenever I engaged whomever it was regardless of the location of the facilities or level of experience in this field.

When I was able to dissect one of the primary sources of the problem, I had to adjust my approach in providing training and mentoring to my newer teammates in several ways. I had to eliminate the assumptions I had that they were already made aware that they had to report to me. The second adjustment I made was ensuring that the level of education and training provided established a foundation. I would then be able to build upon this foundation based on the type of learning capacity that individuals exhibited. Third, I had to understand the internal dynamics and politics of the facility. For example, I had to figure out if other external or internal factors that could slow down the learning process existed. Finally, I had to relate to their frustration of finding out that a new work function was "placed on their laps."

Empathizing with the associations and their displeasure was key to building a strong rapport. Rather than immediately provide training, I would reach out to them slowly through email or if a situation requiring my assistance arose, I took the necessary time to help ease their confidence into a positive frame of thinking. I encouraged the individual to reach out at any time if assistance was needed, and treated their calls and emails with high priority because I know that the most time spent on addressing a situation would be with them because of their lack of comfort and understanding on how to proceed operationally.

The change of strategy yielded strong results. By adjusting to my observed variables, I was able to build a solid rapport with each of the new associates, and that rapport still exists to this day. Even the ones who were quick to profess that was not their job and other trepidations relented after time. Even though I was not too concerned about likeability, I encouraged them to speak freely and allow them to vent. In return, the most resistant began to comply to the point where the lag in providing reports decreased and communication improved.

Knowing and understanding the tangible and intangible barriers that exist in your environment play a critical role in your ability to adjust, adapt, and move forward. As technology and other processes increased performance times to meet organizational requirements, we cannot spend too much time being bogged down trying to resolve old problems. Instead, as a dynamic leader, you demonstrate the capability of recognizing without relying heavily on analytics where the core problems exist and develop the ability to adjust utilizing all your skill sets to move the issue forward.

Sometimes we have to learn how to be comfortable being uncomfortable. Every problem or situation does not have a simple solution. Despite the solution provided in my personal example, I am acutely aware that being the harbinger of change is not an easy task. There is a time when the challenges that come with our current position require time to resolve. However, the mental resiliency must be there to overcome while still attempting to move forward. Your mental resiliency should be high under your Mental Fit. If you do demonstrate a high level of resiliency, you will more than likely provide more than enough motivation for your teammates to follow your lead.

The final exercise under the Mental Fit, Worksheet #3, addresses situations where you identify where you could adjust, adapt, and move forward. This exercise is an exercise of testing your mental resiliency. Before commenting on how you will adjust and adapt, you are asked to identify three situations where you encountered a test. Ask yourself what did you do to make that mental adjustment. Did this action work? If you could face the situation again, what would you do differently?

As a dynamic leader, you will encounter situations where similar circumstances exist. Analogous to no two snowflakes being alike, the situations you face as a leader will not be identical. Despite this fact, some similarities or patterns could be easily identifiable from previous experiences wherein you apply those lessons to the current situation.

Learning and understanding what occurred in the past create opportunities for a brighter future. A significant portion of the repository of information stored in your mind comes from your actual experiences. To put this in simpler terms, imagine that you are responsible for providing training to 40 front-line supervisors about a policy review. The first time or two, with little experience, you are relatively nervous. You spend the evening before worrying about your preparation. Everything, including what you plan to wear, is double guessed. Fast forward to 15 training seminars later, you become an expert in not only the presentation but the preparation itself.

The Mental Fit is the first Fit introduced in this book to assist you in developing a healthy mindset in addressing critical issues that could be in numerous areas. Demonstrating control and patience in resolving these critical matters helps provide clarity and communicates confidence to your team. The three axioms under this Fit are closely related to each other to underscore the foundational aspects of each Fit, and to assist you in connecting the dots holistically. The interchangeable nature of each axiom, as well as each Fit, makes transitioning easier regardless of the type of personality, years of experience, or industry knowledge you currently have.

CHAPTER 3

THE EMOTIONAL FIT

THE MENTAL FIT emphasizes the ability to maintain the mental balance and control. Becoming conscious and fully aware of your external and internal environment takes time and patience. Your ambitions, vision, and desires will not completely align with your team or those who work for you. Therefore, you must demonstrate an ability to be not only a strong leader by example but a strong communicator.

The second Fit under the Four Fits is the Emotional Fit. The Emotional Fit is as it sounds, it addresses the emotions of the dynamic leader. The emotions and the ability to connect with others around us is a trait that is inherent, as well as one that can be learned. If I could use one word to describe the entire context of the Emotional Fit, the word is "will." You must have the will, desire, and passion for becoming great. You must also have the will to overcome adversity whether it is in the workplace or your personal life.

From time to time throughout this Fit, an ongoing discussion about the bridge between your business world and personal world occurs. This conversation is necessary because you are a human being filled with emotions, a personal life, different outside interests, and for some, a family. It is important to remember the keep the balance between the two, and learn how to disengage from the offices, hotels, conventions, and meetings, and appreciate the finer things in life. A theme discussed in both Four Fits books brought up often is your ability to enjoy your life and take time for yourself.

The importance of this Fit as related to a sports analogy is appropriate to use. Your control of your emotions and your ability to empathize with other within your organization opens different paths of communication, improved understanding, and an ability to guide a team through adverse times. There will be numerous times when you feel tested whether you are fostering change, encountering change, or addressing personal circumstances while maintaining stability within your organizational culture. During those times, you will feel pressure, anxiety, stress, and uncertainty. It is natural to feel some levels of anxiety and uncertainty. Your ability to navigate through some of these pitfalls outlines how dynamic of a leader you are.

I am long of the belief that your emotions, and your ability to control them, dictate how active and dynamic of a leader you are or will become in the 21st century. We must continue to keep in mind, as stated earlier in the book, that the culture of the organization or workplace changed from decades ago. Management styles have changed dramatically. Words such as empowerment and autonomy are part of our organizational lexicon. Due to significant advances in technology, more people are working remotely in locations hundreds and sometimes thousands of miles away from their corporate offices.

Such advances in technology create a feeling of independence and self-worth psychologically to our associates and teammates. In addition to how technology changed our world, interactions and communication are more frequent due to various means of communication. Therefore, our associates are mostly psychologically wired for stimulation in some shape or fashion. As leaders, we must be cognizant of those needs and provide the means to keep our associates engaged and motivated.

Although the preceding paragraphs focus on those who are following our lead, we must understand how our personal emotions dictate our ability to lead in the workplace. For the high performing, high functioning managers, it is easy to be swept away from the organizational and operational objectives outlined in predetermined intervals. Sometimes we become so absorbed in our metrics that we fail to take an internal check of our own emotional and mental health. Failure to monitor your general well-being is not only harmful for you physically, it can also negatively affect your ability to lead, motivate, and inspire.

The next three axioms of the Emotional Fit focuses on your capacity to keep your emotions in check and balance. Remember that the purpose of the Four Fits is to help achieve balance. Balance is important no matter what we do or what we are attempting to achieve. If you are a person who appreciates statistics or analytics, you may agree that too much of one thing over another creates an imbalance which could leave to statistical anomalies or errors. As leaders, even though mistakes can happen from our decision-making or actions, we are better served if our decisions are relative and complete in perspective.

Before we dive into the next three axioms, ask yourself why did you want to lead? What sense of personal fulfillment would you achieve by inspiring and challenging others on a regular basis to perform consistently at a high level? Before you read this book, how did you rate yourself as not only a dynamic leader, but as an individual? Even if we continue to strive to be dynamic leaders, we must continue to take heed of who we are as people, appreciate the journey we faced along the way and learn how to reset and recharge our batteries to address the challenges that lay ahead.

Axiom #4: Never forget where you come from

We come from different walks of life, backgrounds, and experiences. Our childhood and the environment that we were around, for better or worse, helped shape our perceptions, biases, and ideologies. Some of us are late bloomers; while some were fortunate from the beginning. Regardless where we are currently in our roles, whether it is for an organization, non-profit, or corporate, we must never forget where we come from.

This axiom has a personal aspect to me as well. If you had the opportunity to read my first book, *The Four Fits of Holistic Growth,* I was relatively forthcoming about some of the experiences I had during my journey to obtain my doctorate. It was not an easy journey. I had my struggles, and I had my demons. That was the personal element. Then there is the professional element.

When I entered the workforce, I was very raw and full of energy. I had a hard time stringing consistency together. Not so much about production, but personality. For whatever reason, that energy continued to get in the way. Sometimes I still believe it cost me opportunities for promotions, and wage increases, but I was determined and ambitious. That ambition helped me in some ways, but in several aspects, it did not. However, I would never trade those experiences because it helped shape me to become the man and the leader that I am today.

You have a fonder appreciation of what you accomplished and where are you are presently if you have encountered adversity. My adversity is different from yours; however, it is not my place nor anyone else to diminish another person's perception of adversity. I entered the workforce at 19 years old as a customer service representative for a private Unemployment Claims Service company. From there, I went to the federal government and worked for five years before being laid off due to a reduction in force.

I stop at this point to state that this was a pivotal moment in my life and professional development. At the time, I had a good government job with benefits at the age of 24. I had talent and ability, but I was not the total package. I laugh as I say that because when the person who told me this I vehemently disagreed with this comment; however, she was correct. I felt that my natural talents and ability were more than enough to take myself to the next level to the sense where I felt entitled to have whatever I wanted. I had experienced my first serious taste of my humble pie. I realized that I had to transform myself to achieve my goals of being successful professionally and financially. To this day, I credit her as one of the integral pieces of my professional development, as well as model some of her leadership traits in this book.

The next two jobs, somewhat related in position and industry, helped improve and polish areas where I was sorely lacking. Without a solid mentor available, I was left to languish on my own. Yes, I had supportive people in my corner; however, I am confident most of us may relate when I say that it is beneficial to have someone that has similar skill sets who can help see you through when you are still relatively green.

During this transformational period, I met some clients who taught me a lot directly and indirectly. Some I consider as good friends to this day where I can pick up the phone and continue to lean on their professional and emotional support. I recall applying for numerous positions, and then I got a call from someone interested in me. He hired me into a position where I had no "direct" managerial or supervisory roles, but he recognized the ambition and determination I had. I recall telling him that if he hired me, he would never regret it. I also call him a friend, as well as a mentor.

This trip down memory lane sets the table for this axiom. While employed by this company, I held numerous duties and responsibilities, but what you did not see in the job description is that you have to be a leader. As a sidebar, I do not name companies or individuals due to confidentiality and respect. When I first started the position, I made a flawed assumption which was that I assumed that others had some fundamental knowledge of the area of specialty I was responsible at that company. I began to administer a series of policies and procedures after reviewing the financial figures that continued with the same assumptions.

Due to these incorrect assumptions, there was some pushback and some personality clashes. After a while, it became painfully apparent that effective leadership cannot exist unless you can have leadership <u>and</u> management become interrelated in ideologies and actions. Despite my goals of reducing costs and expenses, it would be tough to accomplish these goals unless I was able to establish the foundation.

During my epiphany of sorts, I flashbacked to all of those meetings and conferences where expectations were laid out, but my co-workers and I did not understand the basis of change or fully understand the expectation of management. From that point forward, I ensured that I spoke to those under my leadership with varying levels of understanding and inquired as to how could I become a more competent trainer or communicator of my expectations.

The feedback was great and very useful. From that point forward, I removed underlying assumptions and provided training and development from the most basic principles. From the point of engagement with any new staff to clearly communicating expectations, whether verbal or electronic, the team operated at a more efficient level. Their levels of understanding increased and reporting improved, communication improved, and our rapport improved. To this day, when I engage clients, I inquire as to what their needs are, and their level of understanding. Learning how to be in sync with my client's psychological and operational requirements still is paramount in building relationships and producing quality results.

Under the third axiom of the Spiritual Fit, I mentioned that to be great, you have to elevate those around you to be great. Regardless of the type of organizational structure, industry, or dynamics of your company, teamwork plays a significant role in achieving its defined greatness. When we are promoted or hold a distinctive title, it is easy to forget the holiday hours worked while others were salaried and had those coveted days off. We tend to forget all the hard work and perseverance it took to continue to grow in our industry or organization.

Sometimes when we become too far removed from our beginnings, we lose sight of the clearer picture. What we may not even realize from time to time, as discussed earlier, is that someone is looking up to you. These individuals are following your lead because you provide them hope and opportunity. Whether that opportunity stems from inside the organization or without, you are providing a template or blueprint of what it takes to become a dynamic and exceptional leader.

Most of us progressed to where we are today because of a mentor. I call them markers because I would measure my level of success or progress to where they were then. If they were close in age but were further along, I would try and understand what they did to maneuver to their positions. I asked them numerous questions and watched their mannerisms when they spoke or how they provided real leadership when adversity was apparent. Even to this day, I still find those who unknowingly motivate me in a positive way. Just imagine who is watching you now, and who could benefit from your mentorship, leadership, and guidance.

For those who were in sports or watch sports, recall the conversations from how the superstars harken back to their beginnings. Even though they are professionals and reached the highest level of their sport, it is not uncommon to recall the old practices, speeches, and universal principles espoused by their former coaches. Some not only remember their high school coaches, but some also go all the way back when they were in their respective youth leagues. Despite their greatness, they understood that it all started from somewhere.

Consider this axiom as an emotional investment. An emotional investment you place into your team to help achieve their level of greatness. Sometimes, there are some who have that innate drive and competitiveness to succeed. However, there are some who have a latent ability and are not capable of reaching their peak without being motivated or persuaded how unique and talented they are. Remember, you are a dynamic leader, it is your duty to inspire and motivate. You should not feel threatened by the success of others. Instead, you should feel compelled to instill that seed of achievement in those who are in need of such to help energize your team, and possibly yourself.

An emotional investment provides a relationship between your staff and yourself that benefits all involved. For starters, trust is instilled and maintained. Establishing trust helps improve communication, clarity, and commitment to the overall goals and objectives. Building trust is another example of to how the Four Fits are interrelated and interchangeable.

Second, being emotionally invested in the well-being of your staff improves production and strengthens brand recognition. In this era, wages have been relatively stagnant for years; therefore, there must be other ways to keep your team engaged if a financial motivation is not present. If your team has buy-in into the brand, product, or service provided, it shows in their attitudes and actions. A benefit of traveling from client to client is to see the difference of prevailing attitudes of the team. The analytics reflect the performance tied to their overall satisfaction.

Third, becoming emotionally invested in your team creates a self-awareness and improves social skills by managing relationships between your team and yourself (Ovans, 2015). Recall some of the more recognizable leaders from presidents, prominent business leaders, and celebrities demonstrating an ability to connect to those seeking someone to inspire them and someone to relate. Even though their policies and their legacies will always be debatable, it is not hard to argue their ability to connect to those who elected them and continued to support, hope, and believe in their messages.

Before completing the next exercise, I encourage you to take a trip down memory lane. We all started somewhere and reached to where we are today. During that particular journey, for most individuals, the route provided potholes, roadblocks, and other unwanted obstacles. To achieve your defined level of success, you struggled or experienced some form of a setback.

For those who are reading this axiom and planning the next move, you may still find yourself seeking a mentor. With the advances in technology and different means of connecting and networking, a mentor could be someone you know personally or someone you know virtually. To this day, I still seek and find my mentors whether they know it or not to build upon the foundation I created. At the same time, I attempt to chart my path and future goals in line with that mentor.

This form of benchmarking is useful in that it fuels the competition, innovation, and clearly defines your professional goals and objectives. Benchmarking in leadership provides additional opportunities to learn and implement evolving social norms, conflict resolution, and improved negotiations. Under most strategic management courses and concepts, businesses must be willing to continue growing to be aligned with the competition to secure competitive advantages, improved market share, and profitability. Similar concepts apply to dynamic leadership when embracing the evolution of the character, persona, and the will to lead.

Being able to connect your past to your present while establishing the path for your future provides holistic balance in your personal and professional lives. Your ability to form a bridge between the three temporal elements provides a temperament in the administration of your leadership style and persona. As stated before, your team looks up to your leadership, intellect, and guidance to help achieve the operational objectives and organizational culture.

By clearly defining who you are as a person and providing that connectivity to your staff, you establish empathy and compassion. As you continue to develop rapport with your associates, forming a structure that is conducive for your environment benefits all parties involved. The ongoing connection stems from your ability to relate and to not forget where you come from in the beginning.

For Worksheet #4, you are tasked to flashback to the past, examine your present, and determine your future. The key in this exercise is to recall critical moments when you felt as if your career or professional path in life changed. What moments did you experience that helped shape your leadership ideology? Often, we are asked to recall management theories and philosophies. However, we sometimes forget the interpersonal elements of leadership, which includes the ability to look from within as you exert your style of leadership.

Similar to the other axiom exercises, there is not one precise, correct answer. There may exist numerous examples, people, or events that helped shape who you are professionally, and that lasting imprint creates a new legacy inside you. Recall several speeches from politicians over the past 10 – 15 years. Often it is not the words that resonate with the crowd; often, it is how he or she was able to connect and relate to the message provided.

Dynamic leadership follows a similar path. If you become immersed with your analytics and statistics, you lose the ability to connect with your team. Your team is not made up of numbers or trends. Your team consists of a collection of individuals striving to perform numerous different functions to provide a quality good or service. As a leader, your job is to help them stay on task, communicate and become part of the message, as well as part of your team. All this is possible if you improve your ability to relate.

Axiom #5: Understand your work-life balance

You received that promotion or made the career move that you wanted. You move into a management or leadership role within the organization and are eager to enact change. Filled with ideas and enthusiasm, you look forward to the challenges to prove your worth within the organization.

Different motivations exist for those seeking leadership roles. For some, it is about the financial rewards. For others, the prestige and inherent power that comes with the change in responsibility is exhilarating. Regardless of the motivation for the desired change, responsibilities and expectations increase. The cumulative weight of decision-making in leadership roles become more apparent over time. For many, there will be numerous sleepless nights and dreadful Sunday nights prior to beginning the new work week.

Leadership is an ongoing process. No matter what you feel that you bring to the table, you are always a work in progress. Despite the accomplishments you have to date, you will always be in a perpetual state of learning. No matter how many degrees you attained, there will always be someone who has more knowledge than you. Leadership is an exercise of survival, and an exercise of the strength of wills.

The mental and emotional toll of leadership is heavy. To some, the accumulating stress and restless nights may negatively affect your health. Although companies have 40-hour work weeks, often the hours extend to 50, and for some 60. During the winter months, it is not uncommon to see darkness in the morning when going to work, as well as coming home.

Different positions have different responsibilities. With those responsibilities come an unbalanced work schedule, and rigorous demands that most people do not have to manage. Therefore, it is unreasonable to state whether someone should work 60 hours in a work week because I am not privy to what other people do in their positions, nor have I carried the level of responsibilities that some of you have who are reading this book.

However, I am here to tell you that you must have balance. You may accumulate all the financial rewards or bonus points; but, you may never enjoy it if you do not know how to decompress and learn how to unplug from work from time to time. How often have you, or someone you know, worked so much and so hard that they did not know how to enjoy themselves when given free time.

The purpose of this axiom is to underscore the importance of achieving a work-life balance that is beneficial for you. A dynamic leader is not only capable of addressing the travails of work. A dynamic leader is capable of shifting from one gear (work) to another (life) fluidly. Your ability to reach a sustainable work-life balance is beneficial not only for you but some of your decision-making skills as well.

Before determining your work-life balance, you must ask yourself this question: What is your definition of success and what are you sacrificing personally to achieve your definition of success? Sometimes we become so consumed with work; we often forget the sacrifices we ask of others around us, or simply sacrificing our sanity to achieve success.

The majority of you who are reading this are likely Type A personalities. A deep-rooted desire to be successful and leave no stone unturned often fuels your drive. We fear failure, but how often have we considered that we fear success? Pause and think about this for a moment. Are you so consumed with trying to be successful that when you do achieve a certain level of success as defined by your goals set years ago, you find yourself unsatisfied?

Sometimes it is easy to lose sight of what our original goals were from the beginning. We start with a straightforward and easy wish list:

achieve a particular position and obtain a specific salary. Despite these simple goals, we have a desire to have more. We tell our friends and loved ones that we would not mind reaching a certain point professionally and financially; however, the lure becomes stronger to achieve greater.

If you are not balanced, you will become out of sorts. Think of this statement in reverse. Imagine you have been out of work for quite some time. The moment you return to the workforce, imagine the drive and desire you possess in working day to day. Despite the determination you have inside to perform well, you may try to overcompensate based on the pressures of wanting to perform well. Some of this derives from not having a routine waking up during the week and performing the many tasks and duties you had in your previous employment.

Your drive and desire relating to your leadership position put you in a similarly precarious position. The excessive amount of energy you give towards work makes achieving rest more difficult. Even when you find yourself unwinding, you continue to consume yourself with the events of your work day.

The sacrifices that you make exhibiting this particular type of behavior places a strain on your health, relationships, family, and friendships. How often have you found yourself feeling isolated from your friends because you were so consumed with work and not maintaining regular contact with them, that it becomes difficult to re-establish those relationships.

Establishing a work-life balance creates a complete and holistic balance in your life. Despite your professional motivation for success, taking care of your personal obligations, as well as yourself should be as much as a priority as trying to complete a project before the deadline. Despite the increase of responsibility in our professional worlds, especially as we become more successful and accomplished, the more we tend to neglect our personal or familial obligations.

A 2014 study published in the Harvard Business Review depicted the contrasting differences of maintaining work-life balance based on gender and how it disrupts the home dynamic (Groysberg & Abrahams,

2014). For men, who tend to embrace the "good provider" mentality, less time is spent with their families and children to provide opportunities that may not have existed when they were younger. Women, who do not necessarily focus on the provider role as heavily as men, are faced with the stigma of not being available for their children or family responsibilities. As women tend to be more empathetic individuals and provide the most nurturing towards her children, success attained may pull away the quality time most women are culturally expected to provide to their children.

As someone who was a road warrior for his job, I can personally relate to the difficulties of maintaining a family and the demands of my job. I often traveled 60-75% of the time, the majority of the time in a car. Despite the majority of those days away, I realized how easy it was to lose balance in managing my work responsibilities and keeping my home life stable. During the week, my children had numerous sporting events and activities that I would often miss. However, whenever I was home, I made sure that I kept some semblance of normalcy by attending as many practices, games, and events. By doing so, I ensured that I continued to spend as much quality time at home despite the customary fatigue and being road weary.

Learn how to spend the majority of your day and evenings not being consumed with work. Once you are away from work, you should make it a priority to try to unplug from work mentally. Even though we unplug from our laptops and smartphones, sometimes the mind is still engaged and consumed with work. Sometimes we do not even realize that we are talking about work so much outside of work until your significant other or friends bring it to your attention. Even though work is important for a variety of reasons, your interactions with others outside work are equally important.

The same amount of energy you expend on your job, I recommend that you exert the equal, or even more, outside of work. Even if you do not have children or not involved in a relationship, you should always keep in mind that you only live once. What is the point of accumulating all the benefits of your hard work if you do not take the time to enjoy time for yourself?

Achieving a work-life balance helps you manage stress. The effects of stress can be debilitating to the heart, body, and mind. If you do not take the time to remove yourself from stress, your concentration will lapse. Some of the decisions you make while stressed may not be as sharp as you are if you are coming to work relaxed. Built up tension may create conflict in your interpersonal relationships with work, customers, and even your stakeholders.

Often, when I speak to others about what they consider as fun or relaxing, many have a hard time identifying a hobby. Often many do not mention spending time with their children or loved ones as a top five activity. It is unfortunate as people become so consumed with work that they forget the reasons why they are working.

An element of becoming a dynamic leader is to learn how to live. Establishing a hobby, activity, or something that is peaceful and relaxing helps take away the stresses from your occupation. Despite all my travels, I still find time to take time out for myself. My mind is not 100% consumed with work, the next project, the next book, or next great idea. Sometimes, I prefer to find a park or a lake and sit there and zone out, listening to all the sounds around me and focusing on my breathing, somewhat in meditation. Doing so often helps clear my thoughts and resets my mind to move forward to the next task.

You do not always need to take a special vacation to escape the stress from work. As we are compelled to schedule activities for our workday, we should ensure that we spend as much time organizing activities in our personal lives. Those who do take the time to enjoy the pleasantries of life tend to feel recharged when returning to work. We often spend so much time consumed with work that we fail to take care of ourselves the way that we would do a particular project.

Sometimes we become so consumed about our success that we often do not take a step back and note the accomplishments made to date. The drive for success starts by identifying a set of goals. Once we achieve those goals, it is natural to start thinking of a new set of objectives. As you continue to accomplish what you set to achieve, you become so absorbed in your professional goals, that you start to ignore yourself.

Achieving and maintaining success is difficult and challenging at times. As leaders, there are numerous sleepless nights, anxiety, and other feelings that cause us stress. If you feel that this describes you, you should strive to become a more dynamic by embracing adversity with an open mind. Too often, I have observed other leaders become self-absorbed or overthink a situation when a simpler solution exists.

Maintaining an exercise routine or schedule helps decompress your mind from stress. Even if you are too pressed for time to obtain a gym membership, walking or running helps lower the amount of stress you build up in your body. We are all too familiar with the effects of stress; however, many of us do not seek the time to manage it.

Worksheet #5 focuses on how you equate work-life balance despite the rigors of your daily grind. In this exercise, you are to think about five hobbies you enjoy. Keep in mind that this exercise is all about you. This exercise has nothing to do with your organization's mission, goals, or vision. As stated before, no matter how successful you are or will be, you must take the time to incorporate downtime for yourself.

If you have children or a family, I encourage you to spend as much time as possible with your family and loved ones. It is understandable that we work and ascend in our careers to provide for those near and dear to us; however, you should be able to take a step back and appreciate not only where you are today, but appreciate the foundation that you are laying for your future.

Axiom #6: For every cause, there is an effect.

In management, we often reference different flow charts, histograms, and Pareto charts. We use these charts as templates or road maps to the chart's purpose. An organizational chart shows the structure of the organization, as well as reporting structures. Charts utilized in project management help determine critical path methods. Fishbone diagrams are used to help perform a root cause analysis in problem-solving. These charts help draw distinct lines as to the who, what, where, how, and why of analytics.

Leadership does not have a definitive playbook. There is no perfect way to handle every situation, challenge, or adversity faced; however, your actions define your value. Not only is this applicable towards your relationship with your peers, but this also applies to your relationships with your associates within the organization. The ongoing challenge or question you should ask yourself each day is how do other expect you to lead?

To further break down the question mentioned above, consider what leadership entails. You cannot lead or be in charge if there is no one to follow. You cannot provide guiding principles or direction without others on your team. In numerous conferences and networking events, I rarely hear people mention how their team enhanced the company or the individual. Instead, the discussion is relatively negative as it relates to others because someone did not execute or perform their tasks appropriately.

As this axiom relates to dynamic leadership, one should understand that such leadership displays traits of a symbiotic relationship and an understanding of the dynamics of the organization. Organizations continue to become more sophisticated over the years. As a result, the old tried and true methods of yesterday may not suffice in this current environment. As evolution exists within the cultural dynamics, leadership should be willing to demonstrate the same ability to evolve along with their internal and external environment.

Leadership is a symbiotic relationship between the leader and followers (Heremuru, 2008). This particular symbiotic relationship is enhanced by the evolving relationship within each dynamic, particularly within the followers. Promoting effective leadership includes a leader willing to demonstrate the ability to key in on fluctuations displayed by associates. As the overall mood or tone changes, a dynamic leader should show not only the ability but the temperament to adjust to the tone of the organization. Failure to do so could result in losing the resulting message.

Under dynamic leadership, you should be able to understand that despite your perceived or earned position of authority, there will virtually be a subset of different cultures within the larger cultural environment. Such complex cultural environments are evident within the service industry. I note this because more organizations are becoming more service-oriented regardless of the final product or output created by the organizational system.

For example, an associate has worked for the organization for more than 15 years. The associate receives respect from not only her peers but also from other members of management, as well as their customers. When she is not at work, even for vacation, the customers expressed concern as to her well-being. Due to her longevity and charisma, she has appropriated quite a following.

Unfortunately, an investigation concerning some improprieties occurred. The investigation ultimately revealed that this particular associate was the cause of the improprieties. According to your company policy, you are compelled to terminate the associate. A discussion occurred amongst other members of your leadership team before making the final decision. Despite her popularity, energy, and significant contributions to the organization, you ultimately decide that termination of her employment rather than placing the associate on a final reprimand or leave without pay.

Although scenarios will be discussed more in detail later in the book, an unpopular decision occurred. The termination begins the sequence of cause-and-effect, along with the symbiotic relationship evolving with other associates within the organization. I am confident that the majority of us have seen this script play out before. The resulting action of terminating such a beloved and respected associate may never be accepted.

Leadership requires us to make the difficult choices and establish a standard that others must adhere to follow. Although the guiding principles of this axiom, and the entire book, is not about creating a dictatorship; setting the tone, pace, and tempo is paramount to creating boundaries and defining the culture of the organization.

The resulting effect of the termination may not be well received and may be emotional to some staff associates. However, empathy and compassion are emphasized traits in this situation. Despite some of the rigidness established by company policies and the need for consistency, the same company policy does not outline how you address staff or move over from someone considered as a family member to other teammates. As a dynamic leader, the ability to be flexible and sensitive to the situation does not take away your inherent power; however, it maintains and sometimes strengthens the relationship with your associates.

Recall the axiom relating to the three C's: clarity, communication, and commitment. Each principle has a common theme which is the interpersonal relationship between at least two parties. You cannot send a message unless there is someone else to receive the message. The same concepts apply to this axiom as there are a cause and effect for essentially every action relating to leadership and management.

For example, you are a manager for a restaurant. You are responsible for staffing and ensuring that your inventory is current. One weekend, there is a major event going on, and your restaurant is on prime property and anticipating a high volume of visitors. According to forecasted projections, you are projecting a 60% increase in sales more than a typical weekend.

That weekend, you realized that your schedule is woefully inadequate as it was similar to that of your previous weekends, where activity is not as high. You also did not have an appropriate inventory level as well. To add to the mix, you were not aware of the staffing levels until the morning of the event because you did not elect to double-check to make sure that you had adequate staffing levels set.

The entire weekend was chaos. Not only were you short-staffed, but you also found yourself working in different areas to assist your team. The crowds and wait time, which were anticipated to be approximately 15-30 minutes longer than usual, began to push into the 45-75-minute range. As you are short staffed, the orders took longer to process and serve to the customers. More customers were visibly upset, and some customers got frustrated and left because the wait times were longer than anticipated. Staff also became angry in a visible and sometimes vocal manner because they did not understand why they were so short for such a busy weekend.

As the manager, you are responsible for displaying strong leadership and communication. Informing the team before the start of the shift that the weekend may be challenging, or that other options exist is critical. Due to inadequate staffing, more mental mistakes from staff occurred which included less than clean dishes, incorrect orders, and the incorrect orders being returned and still coming back wrong. Regardless of what prevented you from looking at staffing or prepping for the weekend, the cause of the chaos started with failing to be adequately prepared and poor communication with your team. Poor communication contributed to the varying levels of adversity, and the effect was the lack of sales, customer complaints, and disgruntled staff.

Every decision you make or do not make is a catalyst for the resulting action for your operations. Despite the numerous management books, charts, and other reference materials you receive in college or formal training, the negative events stemming from that particular moment derive from failing to utilize common sense. Sometimes, we make simple choices complex when the best route is the direct route.

Worksheet #6 requires you to come up with three different scenarios featuring cause-and-effect responses. The natural inclination while completing this exercise may compel you to think of three negative scenarios. I encourage you not to do so. Instead, think of three different scenarios positive, neutral, and negative. Remember, developing and sustaining a holistic style requires balance. You cannot achieve balance if you are not willing to examine yourself internally and externally from a balanced viewpoint.

In summary, the Emotional Fit encompasses how you are capable of managing your emotions while setting the tone of exceptional leadership to your associates, as well as striking a well-deserved balance for yourself. In numerous conversations that I have had with leaders from different industries, our roles attach a wide array of emotions and feelings. Some are more capable of managing their stress than others. However, I have seen a considerable number of those in leadership roles consumed with their obligations to the point where they possibly are not consciously aware of the energy and overall image they are projecting to their associates and their peers.

These conversations are not heard from a simple question-and-answer format. These observations come from an unsolicited conversation in a variety of settings. If you sat down with a leader and did provide them a question-and-answer format, I am relatively confident that the responses received may sound scripted or politically correct. Learning how to incorporate your personality and character into your leadership role helps strengthen your relationship with your associates. As stated before, you are not trying to become everyone's best friend; however, to lead you are always in a role of an innovator, motivator, and inspiration to others.

Recall the examples of watching political press conferences or those running for high offices. Those who are devoid of much feeling or emotion tend not to excite their base, not because they are not providing solid ideas and policies. Their difficulties in connecting to others stem from their inability to have a relationship with their audience. Different professions, including marketing, sales, and customer service, exhibit traits of establishing relationships to improve their standing. As such, leaders should continue to develop, nurture, and sustain symbiotic relationships with their associates.

CHAPTER 4

THE TEAM FIT

UNDER MOST BUSINESS practices, there exists some form of a relationship model. Relationships exist in a variety of ways. The customer and business model is a common model where an established relationship exists between the customer and the business entity. These customers are known as external stakeholders. Their purchasing power and the organization's ability to market and connect with the stakeholders enhances the relationship. Ongoing rewards to repeat customers, such as in the service and retail industries, encourage a sustainable relationship between both parties.

In a typical management model, a relationship exists between the manager and the employee. In this model, the manager sets the parameters and goals for the employee to complete. These assigned tasks vary from industry to industry; however, communication between the two parties is` effective to clarify the expectations of each employee. The manager is also responsible for evaluation, hiring, termination, and performance reviews, which can positively or negatively affect the employee's relationship with the organization.

Both examples depict stakeholder management as an organization focuses on their external and internal stakeholders. As businesses and the world continue to change and evolve, stakeholder management is increasingly vital. For the purpose of this book, and overall discussion of leadership within an organization, viewing employees or associates as internal stakeholders and your relationship in addressing their needs along with the organization will be the focus.

The stakeholder theory is a theory that addresses morals and values in managing organization (Freeman, 1984). Initial stakeholders under this theory included financial institutions, consumers, government entities, and trade associations. Despite the evolution of the original theory, stakeholders include employees or associates. Employees and associates have a significant impact on overall organizational operations. As more and more organizations became diverse and global, focus on corporate social responsibility grew.

The first two Fits of the Four Fits of Dynamic Leadership focused on the personal aspects of leadership. To become an active and influential leader in the 21st century, leaders must learn how to connect holistically from within and to extend to those who are around the leader. The organizational culture continues to evolve and reflects some of the social themes that permeate our world away from work. These social issues, regardless of the stance you may have towards them, reflect the individuality of those around us who seek identity and acceptance.

Applying some of the concepts associated with stakeholder theory and viewing associates as the internal stakeholders will be the focus of this Fit. Two axioms related to the Team Fit help underscore the unique dynamic relationship between leaders and internal stakeholders. Depending on the nature of your organization, your external target audience, and organizational goals will vary. For some, particularly those in non-profit organizations, providing services to address gaps may be the core objectives. For most companies and organizations, the focus may center on increasing profits, brand management, and increasing market share. Regardless of the overall scope and vision of the organization, the internal stakeholders and the leader's ability to develop and nurture their relationship provides stability and added value within the organization.

AXIOM #7: LEARN HOW TO BE SEEN AND HEARD

Associates, consciously and subconsciously, search for leadership within their culture. Managers and supervisors delegate tasks and evaluate the performance of associates. Despite this being a part of his or her job description, another gear exists in leaders. Dynamic leadership does not come from a company policy or manual. Leadership comes from the ability to connect with others in the organization to lead, motivate, and inspire. Among one of the ways to do so involves visibility.

A difference exists between management and leadership. If you are fortunate to be in a management role, understand that effective leadership is as equally important as going over timesheets to see if your associates are reporting to work on time. As a manager, your primary role includes directing, controlling, planning, and directing. As a manager, that is a title that you may have attained through promotion or other means of employment; however, leadership does not require a title.

Managing by walking around is a concept rooted in ensuring that you are visible to your associates, and ensuring that their tasks are completed. Even though visibility is the goal of managing by walking around, leadership involves being engaged and in tune with your associates. Asking associates, not only about how their day is going, but entering into a dialogue about something that both parties have a common interest encourages ongoing communication. For example, you may walk into two associates talking about last night's football game. Entering into a conversation about the game serves as an ice-breaker, and provides the associates an opportunity to make a connection with you.

You are an administrator for a long-term care facility. Among the numerous duties involving short and long term care, dietary, and other operational oversight, you are responsible for the well-being and morale of your associates. Working for health care operations can be challenging as staffing levels are dependent on the overall census. If the census is low, hours decrease and staff risks losing pay. Furthermore, the external stakeholders, which involve family members, can be challenging as they may not have an in-depth understanding of the amount of work and effort provided in caring for their loved ones. As such, the complaints and demands from family members can be a grind to your associates.

The temperament of your staff begins with you as a leader in this situation. In this particular environment, staff may benefit by seeing you not only walking around the facility but engaging them in general conversation. The daily grind of an aide or nurse can affect them negatively as they are responsible day in and day out for the same residents. Often, the staff may feel unappreciated and overworked. Also, they may feel that management is not sympathetic to their concerns.

Effective leadership in this situation involves active engagement with your staff. Although there are numerous regulations that the facility must adhere to, the internal stakeholder is one of the most crucial links into your overall stakeholder management. If your associates feel embattled or isolated, morale lowers, and the quality of their work could decrease. The lowering of morale is infectious and debilitating. Finger-pointing and assigning blame increase, and the culture of the organization could become fractured.

High turnover could negatively affect perceptions of someone's leadership abilities. Taking the time to appropriately assess whether someone fits the organizational culture or not is something that is closely monitored by staff. If the perception is that management is quickly bringing people in to have bodies available, the risk of bringing in workers who exhibit poor work ethics and limited value towards longevity in the workplace also could lower morale. Rather than being concerned about having "warm bodies" in the facility, taking the necessary time and care to ensure that a prospective employee is a good fit eliminates the domino effect associated with poor hires.

Leadership by example includes demonstrating the ability to be a skilled communicator. As you may recall under the Mental Fit axiom about communication, being clear and concise in your message sets the tone for others to follow. When walking around your operations, make sure you maintain solid eye contact, as well as encouraging the associates to express any valid comments or concerns they may have. Doing so expands the communication channels between the associate and yourself, as well as underscore your ability to communicate the organizational core values, mission, and vision.

Leading by being accessible allows you to witness any potential opportunities to educate associates if a work process or behavior is not performed to standard. Often when staff makes errors, it is not because they are willfully trying not to do the job correctly. Despite all the training and education provided, on the floor education is more valuable than classroom education. Sometimes during training, certain scenarios and situations are not in the video or manuals. When faced with a particular situation, the associate may make a determination that produces negative results. This notion holds true even if the associate is genuinely trying to make the right decision. Being visible provides your associates the opportunity to ask questions or for you to provide a coachable moment based on your observations.

Leading by example also provides you an opportunity to praise and compliment staff for doing an exceptional job or demonstrating the ability to go above and beyond their routine duties. Recall the previous scenario of being an administrator in a long-term care facility. A nurse was able to provide exceptional customer service to a family who was upset about a particular situation involving their loved ones. Rather than deflecting the blame or becoming somewhat confrontational, the nurse exhibited a sense of responsibility, ownership, and integrity in addressing the situation. Although you will follow up with family members about how to further resolve the situation, you are present to take the opportunity to show appreciation to your staff on the spot. Sometimes, an extra "thank you" and "good job" goes a long way in showing appreciation for the work provided.

Achieving visibility helps develop the prospects of inspiring and motivating your associates to perform at a high level. If you are not visible, and you often remain in your office, it is hard to obtain the most that you can out of your employees. Visibility also creates an image of availability and that you are approachable. Dynamic leadership features an ability to be available and accessible to not only your peers but also to those who you are under your guidance.

Despite the technological advances over the past couple of decades, stress has increased in the workplace. The term "burnout" derives from the conditions associated with the workplace that compel the worker to maintain productivity at a high level for an extended duration of time. Results of burnout could include lack of focus, lack of professional efficacy, and cynicism (Laschinger, Wong, & Greco, 2006). Therefore, effective leadership by becoming more accessible and available to your team, provides a sense of security that you are visibly aware of their work conditions, or the presence to see how the environment is manifesting either towards a positive or negative environment.

Dynamic leadership regarding active visibility may create a culture of higher employee engagement and a catalyst for optimal levels of productivity. As a leader, if you embrace the organizational vision and desired environment, that level of energy will transfer to the employees within that culture. This belief holds true during periods of adversity due to problems with external stakeholders or circumstances beyond your control.

Employees cannot be engaged unless leaders create an avenue of employee engagement. It is that ongoing interaction, somewhat in a circuitous loop, that empowers employees to think independently, but still embrace the organization's core values and beliefs. Leaders must also provide an opportunity for employees to become satisfied with their current position regardless of the challenges that come along with it. Most employees are keenly aware of the challenges and demands of their job when they applied for it; however, it is the culture that is created and maintained by leadership that assists in employee retention.

Recently, there has been a spate of global crises that occurred from terrorism, natural disasters, active shooters, and other occurrences where normal operations or a way of life experiences disruption. Despite the unfortunate circumstances stemming from these events, many individuals exhibited dynamic leadership skills which stemmed from being galvanized through these crises. Thus, the ongoing challenge for leaders is to develop, whether implicit or explicit, a solid communication strategy for employee engagement, empowerment, and direction.

Recall the axiom relating to empathy. To nurture and sustain a healthy communication channel between leadership and associates, exhibiting a sense of empathy and understanding creates some level of trust and understanding between the two parties. As well, it creates an opportunity for new leaders, to develop internally to assist the recognized leader.

When you read this axiom, you may believe that you are visible or that your desired objectives are well-known. The sobering reality comes when you are going over a report or procedure with an employee only to discover that the employee did not have a clear understanding as to your expectations. I vividly recall that my background experience makes communicating my craft to others under my care easy. However, it took a year or two to realize that not only they were not clear as to the procedure; but also did not understand why the system existed.

As a result of this discovery, I changed the way I provided training and communicated to my team. I spent more time in the field just to be available and not associated with auditing or something negative. Building a rapport with my team improved communications both ways, as well as help me develop ongoing training opportunities for those who possibly could benefit if there was policy or procedure that was not clear. Before that moment of clarity, I was not aware that this type of communication was necessary. From that moment forward, communication has increased exponentially, and the team has a deeper understanding as to not only what we are doing, but why.

While completing Worksheet #7, I encourage you to consider your style of leadership. Think how often you lead by example and ask yourself are you a leader who is often seen and heard? When you first start this exercise, you may be surprised that you may not do much leadership by example or have a low level of visibility. Sometimes, we become so wrapped up in reporting, policies, and administration, that we tend to forget about our biggest asset and stakeholder: our employees.

Recall situations where you realized that your presence could provide more of a benefit to your employees. Occasionally, we become so engrossed with what we have to do, we tend not to consider what our employees may need from us. Sometimes the answers to what they need are obvious. Sometimes it may not be as obvious, but remember as a dynamic leader, you always are responsible for ensuring that you get the most out of your employees, yet keep them enriched and engaged into team buy-in.

While completing the exercise relating to this axiom, you will consider ways that you are presently exhibiting your style of being seen and heard. While completing this exercise, think of ways that you could enhance or implement what you are currently doing. Even if you feel that you are doing an exceptional job with your interpersonal skills, one thing to keep in mind is that the organizational culture is always subject to change, just like your industry culture. Including more efficient and fresher strategies will continue to keep your staff engaged and open to your dynamic leadership style.

In conclusion, this axiom summarizes the importance of creating synergy between you and your team. Employees have more responsibilities and tasks to complete than they did decades ago, which could result in burnout, low morale, or high turnover rates. Reviewing reports and statistical analysis may help provide a snapshot; however, the value of understanding human behavior and psyche is as critical as overall production. In this axiom, visibility and engaging your team is strongly encouraged to address any gaps that could be explicitly or implicitly present.

AXIOM #8: A DYNAMIC LEADER HAS A DYNAMIC RELATIONSHIP WITH THE TEAM

If you are one who follows team sports, you see a constant dynamic on championship teams. Taking the coach away from the equation, you have a collection of players who are striving for a championship. The coach is there to provide leadership, strategy, and often is the last voice before play resumes; however, the players are the ones who are on the field of play.

If a team is down, whether it is a goal, touchdown, or 7 points with four minutes to play, the dynamics of the team begin to show. From those close and challenging situations, there is often someone who has been known to rise above the occasion. This dynamic player or superstar is often the one that the team leans on when the situation becomes difficult. The superstar of the team has demonstrated excellence on the field and has been known to carry the team to greatness. This fact remains true whether it is Manning, Brady, Jordan, Kobe, Gretzky, Lebron, or Jeter. These superstars have that extra gear in them and will continue to fight until the game is over.

Even though work is not as extreme as sports, outstanding leaders feature dynamic traits that galvanize the team to follow him or her to excellence. Even though a Super Bowl or NBA Finals is not on the line, the leader is willing to motivate, lead, and inspire by being willing to incorporate many personalities and the temperament of his or her team. Encouraging others to follow your leadership, relationship-building, and management are useful concepts to incorporate into your persona. Before focusing on your relationship management skills, it is important to understand your team dynamics and how it affects the overall organizational culture.

Team dynamics are intangible in nature. In essence, it is the psychological forces that influence a team. These psychological and intangible forces significantly affect the team's behavior and performance (Meyers, 2013). What makes team dynamics unique is how they can either positively or negatively influence the working environment and how they interact with external stakeholders.

Team dynamics may also describe the culture within the organization. Positive or negative energy in an organizational environment influences turnover. If team morale is low, negativity creeps in and spreads like weeds. The energy that should be relatively positive is taken over by mistrust, poor communication, and conflict. If the team dynamics and morale are in disarray, overall individual and team performance are affected. Employees are less inclined to come to work, and for those who do come into work, they may dread or quickly await the end of the day to come.

Unfortunately, negativity speaks larger volumes than the positive vibes that may exist within an organization. As a result, such negativity could affect ongoing business by casting a negative perception of the operation. Qualified and talented potential new hires may be inclined to look elsewhere for employment. In some circumstances, poor morale may inadvertently cause new hires to quit well before their probationary period.

Earlier in the book, I mentioned that statistics do not tell the entire story of the operation. When collectively looking at turnover rates in your region, you should begin a root-cause analysis to determine why such a high turnover rate exists. As an active leader, continue to seek answers analytically as well as personally with others where turnover is the greatest. Meeting with other department heads or others who directly report to you will not provide all the answers you seek. The department heads and those who report directly to you will mostly tell whatever story that he or she may think you want to hear; however, you as a leader will continue to be clueless as to the entire team dynamics.

If you are in a position where you have high turnover rates, what is your current strategy for addressing it? If you are discussing it directly with the person in charge, recall the discussion about communication. The moment you are relaying the message to the receiver, the receiver automatically becomes the sender and communicates the message to his or her team in his or her words. Therefore, the probability of the message being muddied increases, and the original intent of the message can become lost.

I am not advocating for all senior level members of management to be on a first-name basis with the staff at the most basic of positions. However, I do advocate for a way to communicate the importance of unity and sharing the organizational message and vision emphasizing the person who directly reports to you as the focal point of delivering the message to the team. This particular method reinforces the importance of the immediate supervisor to the team, and how the team can galvanize around the supervisor. Also, the visibility sends a message to others about the importance and value of the overall mission and vision of the organization.

One of the underlying and unknown strengths of organizational culture is the understanding of the team dynamics and how to incorporate them as an important stakeholder to overall operations. Improving on the team or group dynamics is beneficial to the organizational mission and vision as performance, communication, information sharing, and trust improve. The members of the team are likely to come to a consensus quicker, and creativity develops as well.

Negative team dynamics undermine the leader's ability to lead. Progressive leaders have the essential skills and abilities to motivate, lead, and inspire. If the dynamics of the team are relatively weak, the message the leaders attempts to communicate becomes muddled, and the intent of the message becomes lost in translation. Negative team dynamics do not necessarily relate to a negative vibe or ongoing gossip; however, the team may instinctively defer to the leader's recommendation. These set of actions create groupthink within the team, and innovation becomes either diminished or lost over time.

The pulse or emotions of the team can either positively or negatively affect the team's ability to accept innovative change or changes to processes or adopting new technologies. For example, if you are the leader championing change about a new emerging technology, and you have a team dynamic that is receptive to the change, the integration, usage, and feedback is positive, and the intended use of the technology may improve. Conversely, if the team is apprehensive to change and there is little to no explanation or planned phased-in changes, the resistance to the new technology will be so strong that delay of implementation of the new technology exists or the overall implementation and usage phase may experience disruption.

Understanding the team dynamics of your organization has several benefits as discussed above. If you have a grasp of what those dynamics might be, whether positive or negative, relationship building or management becomes equally important. Relationship management and emotional intelligence involve your ability to improve, maintain, or nurture a positive environment in the workplace, as well as improve the overall culture of the organization.

The general concept of relationship management involves a connection between leadership or management and the team. As you may recall under the Mental Fit, the previous discussion provided the strengths of the 3C's: Communication, Clarity, and Commitment. That axiom wraps into this axiom and among the other Fits in that your team must not only hear you, but they also need to understand and feel you when you are leading.

As organizations continue to evolve, so does the labor force. Commitments to an organization are shorter-lived than in the past. According to the 2016 Bureau of Labor Statistics news release, the average length of employment tenure was 4.2 years. Of note, the average length of employment tenure dropped from 4.6 years in 2014. The average length of employment varied with the age of the worker. The median length of employment for those classified as older workers was approximately 10.1 years; whereas, the average age of employees 25 – 34 was approximately 2.8 years (BLS, 2016).

The length of employment thus underscores the importance of relationship management, as well as understanding the team dynamics. Depending on the industry, the team may feature a mixture of employees ranging in age, racial make-up, and philosophical beliefs, as well as other factors. Due to the diversity, you find in the workplace, it can be difficult to predict the behavior and prevailing attitudes of the employees around you.

Along with anticipated shortened commitments to an organization, turnover rates are expected to be a constant constraint in maintaining and nurturing the organizational culture. The challenge for leaders is to understand the factors that influence turnover, as well as anticipate the mindset of an associate as you welcome him or her to the organization. As stated before, employees have different motivations for working for your organization. Your task, as a dynamic leader, is to understand and embrace his or her motivation for employment and leverage the existing opportunity in the best manner possible.

The statement above recalls my relationship with one of my supervisors. Even though I affectionately called him "Big Boss," due to his striking resemblance to one of my favorite video game series characters, he emphasized team and had excellent relationship management skills. I recalled one of the first visits in the field wherein we eventually came around to my ambitions and desires as I was in the midst of wrapping up my doctoral studies.

He considered himself a capitalist, and believed that everyone had their right to earn or work wherever they could. I recall him mentioning that on top of my doctoral studies, I would have a "Ph.D. in all things risk management in two years, and people will want your knowledge and skills." Even though I worked well past those two years, and completed my doctorate, he was always supportive of my endeavors, and I felt very comfortable discussing ideas of my next step or ventures I contemplated in exploring.

His relationship with other members of the small team was very positive and well-received as well. Even though the pay could be more than what it was, as well as not receiving raises at times, his leadership, guidance, and willingness to allow us to think and speak freely were very welcomed in an environment that was highly stressful and carried heavy responsibilities. It was one of the chief reasons why I enjoyed working for him and the organization, as he allowed me and my teammates to be ourselves while endearing ourselves to the organizational culture and vision of the company.

In my personal example, his belief of relationship management factored in the background, expertise, and skill set of his team, with the knowledge that any competitor or another organization or industry could pluck us away and he would have to deal with all the travails of turnover. Even though turnover was inevitable in some circumstances, the loyalty I saw from the team, including myself, was something that I rarely saw or observed personally in other workplaces.

Relationship management and team building is an intangible task in your job description as a manager, director, or supervisor. Even though organizations go out of their way to have BBQs, happy hours, or recreational team building events, the before and after the involvement of the leaders outside the team-building activity provided more reinforcement to the overall concepts of the organizational culture.

Relationship management involves your ability to interact and connect with others within your team. There are several ways to improve or increase your relationship management skills; however, the most common denominator is you. You are present and involved with your team in a manner that this book and other books may not be able to translate directly to your organization. Books such as these should enhance or expand your awareness of your leadership skills. Your job is to understand what makes your team ticks and how you can not only just educate, lead, or inspire but enhances your ability to learn from your team, as well as find out more about yourself.

Relationship management, as well as other concepts and axioms discussed throughout this book, is an organic activity. If you find yourself or the organization being static, it is your responsibility as a dynamic leader to infuse some life and energy into those around you. You must continue to remember that we now live in an era of selfies, social media, and in some sense, entitlement. Workers are more than likely to question your decision-making and leadership skills, hopefully in private, as more people feel entitlted to become more opinionated.

If your style of leadership is static and does not feature any traits or signs of evolution, you also affect the organization. Stakeholder management is more than your interaction with your external stakeholders; it also involves the way that your associates interact with your external stakeholders as well. From the perception of the external stakeholders, they will anticipate the politically correct or scripted responses; however, the actions of your associates will likely have a higher chance to leave an imprint on the minds of the external stakeholders than the actions or words you provide. Remember, that once those range of issues become the forefront of your activities, the damage has occurred.

As a dynamic leader, you should always be cognizant of relationship management, team building, and the morale of your associates. As stated before, sometimes we become so engrossed with the analytics we often ignore the numbers that are not on the report, which is our associates who rely on our leadership and guidance. It sometimes starts with how you are educating or administering corrective action where you take the extra couple of minutes to improve your relationship with that particular associate.

Breaking down perceived barriers improves relationship management. Recall the example of the young administrator I counseled about her relationship with her new associates. Being able to walk into a position of operation management and profess that you are in charge is easy to do. However, how you break any barriers that may be present improves communication and improves your relationship with your team.

Sometimes the best method of communication is not to speak. Listening provides some of the best information possible in addressing concerns or potential problems the team may have. If you have an open door policy, do not just state you have an open door policy and begin tuning your associates away because you have other pressing matters. Keep the open door policy as a fair and equitable venue for your associates to discuss their concerns openly or just hear them speak in general.

Listening provides an opportunity to gain the additional respect of your teammates. Even though you cannot guarantee any action or results, listening shows that you care and provides you an opportunity to learn the pulse of the environment which commands respect as you demonstrate an ability to be an active listener.

Listening to your staff needs could further limit turnover. Communication is essential in understanding the tangible and intangible needs of your staff. Furthermore, you can identify ongoing training needs necessary to ensure your team has the necessary resources available to improve work efficiency. Remember, there is a difference between leadership and management. It takes an exceptional individual to become a leader. Often this is the case, regardless of the industry where some of the individuals who have more inherent leadership skills do not get selected for management positions.

Dynamic leadership comes from wanting to be dynamic. Establishing a dynamic connection between your team and yourself provides many tangible and intangible benefits that can improve interpersonal relationships, as well as improve operational efficiency. If you are currently in a position of leadership, keep in mind that every day you establish the tone that your team will follow each and every day. Your ability to demonstrate flexibility will further enhance additional opportunities to draw the best from your associates, regardless of the period of adversity you may face.

In the next exercise, I challenge you to put yourself in the shoes of your associates. Before this exercise, you focused on assessing your leadership abilities from a "looking into the mirror" perspective. Although, it is somewhat difficult to look at yourself in such a fashion, remember the theme throughout this book is the holistic development of your leadership styles in a manner that is dynamic and synergistic to your team that follows you. You could also consider seeking anonymous evaluations from your team, either before or after the completion of this exercise.

To complete Worksheet #8, you may want to ask those within your team to rate your leadership style. Although, your team may be hesitant to respond due to your relationship with personal power, think of scenarios that you may have encountered to see how staff may consider that may be the best alternative in that situation. This type of response may provide clarity and insight into what their expectations is of you in your role, which is as pivotal of the stakeholders you must consider in your relationship with them.

Teamwork is an often used word when it comes to organizational culture and discussing your relationship in your current role with your associates. Despite all the training, videos, and readings, including this book, it is your application of the concepts and lessons learned to true operational settings where you can see how you can improve in areas that you may not be aware that you may have deficiencies. Furthermore, your development as a leader does not cease once you attain a level of professional achievement. The responsibilities you carry increase, the pressure and stress build, yet your resolve should remain firm. Your presence should be approachable and accessible. Your team expects this from you as leaders within the 21st century.

The central point for this particular axiom looks at the importance of team and how it relates to your overall ability to lead. Leadership is not an easy task. Even if you read this book and countless other leadership books, there is no way to predict human behavior accurately. The day to day activities and the unique personalities of your associates create an interesting mix of volatility, serenity, cohesiveness, and calamity. The unknown knowns you encounter on a day-to-day basis demonstrates your ability to be an effective communicator, a trustworthy listener, and a dynamic leader.

CHAPTER 5

PERSONAL POWER FIT

POWER AND LEADERSHIP go hand in hand. As stated numerous times, the overall theme of this book is to accentuate dynamic leadership. A leader should be able to inspire, motivate, lead, manage, and empower. A dynamic leader takes these elements and incorporates the emotional, psychological, and mental dynamics that affect the organizational culture. Regardless of your assigned title in an organization, you have the ability to command others who seek direction and redirect others who may need your guidance whether they acknowledge it consciously or subconsciously.

Recognizing you have power is one thing; however, using it in a manner strategically aligned to the organization along with your personality, as well as the stakeholders you interact with is another. Using a baseball analogy, a closer in baseball is someone who is responsible for making sure that the game ends in a victory. Normally, this closer has a repertoire of pitches but is best known for his 100-mph fastball. In a close game, he does not have command of his fastball as much as he would like, and the hitters are locking into his pitches. As this is a critical game in the championship series, he is the best solution in an attempt to end the game. He ultimately decides to rely on his secondary pitches to save the game.

Even if you are not a fan of baseball or sports in general, this analogy shows that there <u>are days</u> when you are not at your best, however, you are still summoned and required to finish the deal. Sticking to the same pitch or the same style of management and leadership does not always equate to winning results. Establishing your flexibility to demonstrate command is an ability you develop, as you continue to grow and mature as a responsible and dynamic leader.

Use of power can be positive or negative. Understanding the nature of your organization and your relationship within it provides more clarity as to the extent of power you are capable of yielding or at the very least the limits of the power you have. Although you recognize that you have a certain level of power, that does not equate to you being an active or dynamic leader. If you are utilizing your power as an avenue to take advantage of those perceived lesser than you, you are diminishing your skills as a leader, and respect from your peers.

Sometimes power can be abused. The abuse of power comes from the resistance to the core principles of power. In the article, *Leadership as a Function of Power*, a taxonomy of power was explored in detail (Green, 1999). The five levels of power included reward, coercive, legitimate, expert, and referent. The five levels of power address commitment and compliance; however, the resistance elements of each level of power found that hostility, demands, and arrogance can erode the leader's ability to effectively use his or her power (Green, 1999).

Before we move into the two axioms related to this particular Fit, recall how often you heard or know of someone referred to as a leader as someone who "did not have many friends in high school, or was happy at home and is now taking it out on others." Whether this statement is true or not, abuse of power is apparent, as the associates or team feels hostility or feels uneasiness about performing the essential functions of the job.

Recall the axioms of the Team Fit. The primary reason for discussing the Team Fit before the Personal Power Fit is to underscore the importance of team, and how you are the driving force of that team. While some of the more old-school, conservative, and conventional styles of leadership may connect with some, the ever-changing dynamics of those on the team dictate that your leadership style should be capable of adjusting, adapting, and moving forward with the streams of change.

The Personal Power Fit is the final Fit in this entire process of holistic growth because the other three Fits focuses on varying degrees of communication, relatability, and teamwork. If you are solely focused on your position and the power that comes along with it, how can you lead when you do not possess the intuition to use your influence in a manner that is beneficial to all parties involved? This book is not advocating that you should incorporate the "let the inmates run the asylum" type of mentality; however, understanding the value of your internal and external stakeholders enhances the value of your leadership skills and abilities.

As you read the next two axioms relating to the Personal Power Fit, try putting yourself in the shoes of the receiving party. Often, when we are providing direction or even clarifying our intentions to our associates, we sometimes forget that they may not have the same level of understanding as we do. Even though we carry great responsibilities as leaders, we have a moral obligation of understanding the type of power that we wield, and how it can either enhance or delimit your position as a dynamic leader.

Axiom #9: Understand the Tangible and Intangible Characteristics of Leadership

You may recall the discussion about the two types of communication: verbal and nonverbal. Leadership qualities are separated by two different traits as well: tangible and intangible. Even though there are varying degrees of power in leadership, understanding the tangible and intangible qualities of leadership enhances inherent power and can influence your ability as a dynamic leader.

Tangible leadership helps a leader achieve goals and objectives. Establishing strong tangible traits help provide visible ways why your leadership is legitimate and why it can be effective. Your skills and knowledge are leadership traits that should be utilized as often as possible in a manner where your team can trust and believe in your abilities, as well as you.

To effectively have your team follow your lead, technical knowledge is necessary. Even if you are a veteran with the company, always seek to understand more about your industry, as well as the role that you are currently assigned. Most organizations will provide ongoing training or educational opportunities, whether in-house or through external opportunities; however, networking provides added value to your position. With significant technological advances made over the past 20+ years, you are capable of connecting with professionals you may never get a chance to meet, or read information that may not be in your local newspaper or major periodical. Seeking this additional information provides you a fair opportunity to improve your Strengths, Weaknesses, Opportunities, and Threats (SWOT) analysis for your organization.

If you have been with an organization for an extended period of time, you become somewhat insulated from the surroundings of your environment. This type of insulation and isolation may limit your ability to gain additional information within the industry that is beneficial for your ongoing professional development, as well as how to interact with your teams.

Earlier, we discussed some of the negative effects of turnover and some of the related causes. Another source of turnover may not be as explicit as one may think. Slow responsiveness to changes within the industry may inadvertently accelerate turnover. For example, the Great Recession of 2008 withered jobs and wages for an extended period. However, as recent as 2016, wages have increased moderately (BLS, 2016). If an organization continues to operate lean and refuse to provide raises, especially to their rising performers, it is almost inevitable that top talent may leave for something as simple as an increase in pay.

If you are reading this and are in a position of senior leadership, you may look at this brief example and think that workers are expendable. Although this may be true to some extent, your lack of emotional intelligence may hinder your organization in ways that cannot be measured. Innovation, creativity, and flexibility may diminish if your organization continues to lose top talent due to the willingness to hold the line regarding wage increases. If the organization sends conflicting messages by saying that there is not much revenue available for wage growth, but there continues to be expansion in operation, morale also can be negatively affected. Therefore, assess the pulse of your organization, and attempt to rank your internal value of the morale of one of your most precious organizational assets.

Competence is another vital, tangible leadership trait. Previously, skills and knowledge were discussed as tangible leadership traits. All three of these traits are interrelated. I would encourage that if you are interested in working one of these three, you should practice working on the other two traits. Exhibiting high morals and standards, clear communication of expectations, and willingness to be open to new ideas and concepts were qualities that scored high amongst 195 global leaders (Giles, 2016).

Establishing a connection with your associates help provide additional opportunities to educate and engage your associates in more intimate levels. Associates do not necessarily seek to develop a "best friend" relationship with management; however, even at the most subconscious level, a desired level of trust is sought. Establishing a connection with your associates also nurtures growth in those who are seeking it. Remember, reason and need are fulfilled when people report working for your organization. Connecting and understanding their reasons and needs benefit the entire organizational culture.

Leadership features intangible qualities. Recall the axiom concerning communication. There are two types of communication: verbal and non-verbal. Non-verbal communication includes the posture of an individual sitting in a meeting; the way a manager informs the team of who is the employee of the month; or how someone smiles when he or she hears something pleasant. The intangible traits of leadership do mirror non-verbal communication. The subtle or implicit context of how you can lead your associates influences the direction of your organization, as well as establishing the organizational culture.

Intangible leadership traits focus on your core personality traits and your ability to process the pressures, stresses, and accomplishments, which come with being a leader. Some supervisors and managers may not respond well to such fluctuations. Being calm under fire and pressure is a huge step in establishing the tone, pace, and tempo of the organization.

If you polled numerous senior executives, you would encounter different characteristics of intangible leadership. For the context of a discussion of this book, intangible characteristics for dynamic leadership include will, integrity, and insight. Every leader features his or her set of individual characteristics that accentuate their style of leadership. These selected traits are not universal, and based on the depths of your personality; you may find other intangible traits that add value to your style of leadership. Continued development and self-identification bode well for overall growth for your method of leadership, as well as personal growth.

No matter what field or industry you are in, you will encounter adversity, and you will encounter failures. People address failure in a variety of ways. Some may confront their failures directly. Some may try to avoid the aftermath of failures or mistakes. Some may present a strong front in the face of failure but may struggle mightily internally.

Great leaders demonstrate the ability to rebound from failure. It is human nature to feel down or a sense of rejection when a failure occurs. No one wants to feel like he or she is lost. No one wishes to feel like he or she are not good enough. The passion and desire to succeed come from within. The belief that you can bounce back from adversity is what defines a dynamic leader. When confronted with adversity or hardships in the workplace, your staff will look at your leadership and respond positively as a bond is shared showing that you had your team's back when they needed your guidance.

Each day will feature its set of triumphs and tribulations. For every great Thursday you experienced, you will encounter challenges even on Fridays. In your role, no two days are alike. Despite the highs and lows that accompany your role in the organization, your temperament and ability to stay resolute and even-keeled demonstrate composure, calm, and civility to your team. Many aspire to become leaders either with their current organization or elsewhere. However, the sobering reality is that many do not understand or possess the tangible or intangible traits and characteristics of leadership.

Remember that for better or worse, your team or associates will feature an eclectic mix of personalities. Some of your associates come from varying backgrounds and exhibit numerous cultural, social, and fundamental differences. Focusing on the intangible characteristics of leadership, imagine yourself as the center of the solar system. You symbolize the sun, and your associates resemble the planets that orbit around you. Your leadership style has to have some form of centrist mentality to have your associates to continuously intertwined in your proverbial solar system.

To further expand this concept, the planets and moons within the solar system function from the energy the sun emits. The gravitational pull that comes from the sun helps keep the planets within the orbit. The moon continues to react from the gravitational pull from the planet. Despite being the center of the solar system as the sun, each planet exhibits different atmospheric and physical characteristics. However, each planet functions as a member of the solar system. If the sun becomes unstable or volatile, a catastrophic event such as a black hole forms, and consuming everything in its wake.

Although not as cryptic, your existence as a dynamic leader functions as a sort of gravitational force for your team. As stated before, your associates have numerous skill sets and personality traits that make your organization unique. However, to maintain some form of balance and civility, your presence as a dynamic leader helps creates the energy to keep your associates engaged. If you are not in tune with your associates, volatility could occur which creates additional expended energy into the intangible areas of management and operations that do not show up on monthly reports.

Connectivity and maintaining it on a consistent and constant basis is another intangible characteristic of dynamic leadership. As stated numerous times throughout this book, today's workers feature a more open and engaging, as well as a dynamic mix of personalities. You motivate each person who reports to your leadership in a variety of ways that may either directly or indirectly affect their relationship within the organization.

As the average worker becomes more skilled and specialized, the pursuit of educational growth accelerates as a priority, especially for workers of a younger demographic. Rather than looking at that associate as someone who has a limited time within your organization, recognize that he or she is a valuable asset that can assist in fulfilling the organizational vision and mission. Despite his or her career aspirations, ultimately, you are not sure if he or she will remain in the organization long-term. Nonetheless, you should seek to determine a way to incorporate the individual's eagerness to grow into your operational plans.

Your associates are human beings with feelings and emotions. Ultimately, especially those who have been in the organization for quite some time, your associates seek to feel a sense of belonging or purpose. If you are running a healthcare organization, it is reasonable to assume that those who desire to work there want to serve the patients. However, the question is how do you connect with your staff to have them passionately perform at a high level?

Connectivity features your ability to relate the organizational mission, vision, and purpose to one of your most important stakeholders, your associates. Returning to the healthcare example, if you see an aide address a situation that requires him or her to remain professional and calm, you should take the time to acknowledge the associate and thank him or her for the effort in handling the situation. Even if there is a misstep in the manner the aide handled the situation, use it as a teachable moment, and continue to communicate the aide's value to the organization.

When I conduct training throughout the country, I enjoy embracing the role of a teacher, as well as a leader. Despite my title or standing amongst the attendees, I often seek to connect with them early on. This thought process provided me the opportunity to accentuate the message I intended to portray. Even if a particular operation may have had its shares of challenges, I made it an effort to steer away from their challenges. Although everyone in the room knew what the challenges might be, connectivity was important because I always wanted to convey the importance of ownership and accountability.

Even when I conducted audits where I knew that the scores might not be up to standards, I continued to portray confidence in the team in turning their scores around. The way I was able to do so was to take away the focus on the score itself, but to interject how they play a larger role in limiting liability and losses. Often, the results of follow-up audits featured a marked improvement of scores, as well as increased ongoing communication between the team and myself.

Since the Great Recession of 2008, the economic outlook has been unpredictable regardless of the industry. Some industries featured booms, busts, and challenges. Despite the other economic indicators trending upwards, businesses still continue to find creative ways to keep employees engaged and employed within their organization despite the fact that raises were either small or not too common. Again, connectivity is important as an intangible characteristic that can come in play in managing your associates.

I recall one of my managers whom I have a fond and sincere appreciation for since my arrival to the organization. Even though raises were not being frequent or minimal compared to what the industry average could be, he had an uncanny way of connecting not only with me, as I was wrapping up my doctoral journey, but other highly-qualified and diverse employees under his care. The work was not easy, and often stressful; however, his ability to connect to each one of us within the team created a bond where each one of us continued to put forth our best effort no matter what.

His leadership style is something I had decided to emulate as I continued to grow as a professional. It was not the end statistical results that told the story; it was how you were able to connect with others in the field. Recognize the efforts and work that not only the management team put in day in and day out, but also everyone from the housekeeper to the cook in the dietary department. Everyone was important because everyone was there to serve the residents. As I continued to grow and develop my style of leadership, as featured in the Four Fits of Dynamic Leadership, I realized that despite my personal ambitions, servant leadership was very rewarding. The financial rewards would come in due time; however, I realized that during my time under his employ, it was the message that mattered more than the hours I put in on and off the clock.

Thus, this is why connectivity is an intangible characteristic of dynamic leadership. Being able to connect to staff no matter where I traveled provided the intangible values of leadership. From the moment I walked in the door until the moment I walked out, the smiles from the staff matter because it was that period, whether it was two hours or six hours that I was able to project their importance to the overall core vision of the organization.

Regardless of your tenure within the organization or your current title, your ability to consistently perform servant leadership, yet all the while remaining firm and absolute in your role provides more value than the person who obsesses over the figures. I love numbers, data, and statistics; however, being wrapped up in quantitative methodology does not do your team a service because they are not a mere statistic. They are more than the numbers that show up on your labor reports. I challenge you, whether you are operations or not, to understand and connect with your associates to assimilate their daily purposes to your leadership style. For some, making it check-to-check is their primary objective. For others, seeking and fulfilling their career and professional ambitions are more important. Nonetheless, you remain a central force in providing the gravitational pull for their wants and needs, all the while fulfilling the operational objectives you seek to accomplish.

If you conduct numerous surveys with some of the world's foremost leaders, you will have different definitions or perceptions of strong intangible and tangible leadership qualities. Even though there is no precise answer, as evidenced by numerous articles and seminars dedicated to this subject, you should define and establish traits that you feel makes you a dynamic leader. Furthermore, you should be able to understand how both sets of characteristics benefit not only your team but also compliments and enhance them as well. Remember, you are great if your team is great. Therefore, develop the tools or discover ways to further improve your skills as an effective skilled communicator and strengthen your connectivity with your associates.

For the penultimate worksheet, you are to identify, in your own words or research the tangible and intangible characteristics of leadership. Expanding your knowledge and foundation of these characteristics may enhance your leadership skills. I recommend researching online some of the more reputable management journals or business schools renowned for their contributions to the management field. Take the time to consider in what areas you may face challenges to your leadership abilities. Remember, an active and dynamic leader focuses on existing challenges, as well as known strengths. Increasing awareness provides benefits to those who follow your lead, as well as improves communication of your organizational goals and objectives.

Axiom #10: Emotional intelligence is more than common sense

Throughout this book, you have been introduced to the concepts of the Four Fits of Dynamic Leadership. If you carefully review each axiom, you will see a theme of building from within yourself, as well as building your team. Despite the interchangeable nature of the words "team" and "associates", you primarily operate in a world where your ability to effective manage your interpersonal relationships with others improves operational efficiency, improves established lines of communication, and creates a sense of heightened self-awareness within yourself as a dynamic leader.

The final axiom for this book touches on emotional intelligence under leadership settings. Emotional intelligence is an individual's ability to address not only their emotions but also demonstrate an ability to address another person's emotions effectively. Emotional intelligence comes from the capacity to become empathetic and understand how to recognize and effectively label the emotions or feelings of another. With the complex and diverse make-up of employees in the workplace, developing and holding a high level of emotional intelligence improves communication, team-building, and differentiating between leadership and management.

Under the Mental Fit, a discussion of emphatic learning focused on recognizing the feelings and emotions of those under your guidance. Under the Power Fit, you are now extending the conversation of emphatic learning by applying it towards how you interact with your associates in developing and leveraging your relationship with them. In this axiom, discussion of emotional intelligence focuses on three areas: feedback, collaboration, and coaching.

Emotional intelligence is a relatively new concept in comparison to other management concepts and theories. A concept developed in the 1990's, emotional intelligence has received more traction in leadership and management training and discussions. In 1998, Daniel Goleman provided five components of emotional intelligence: self-awareness, self-regulation, motivation, empathy for others, and social skills (Ovans, 2015). In a sense, the Four Fits of Dynamic Leadership in an extended discussion adding to emotional intelligence as the focus of this book is by your continued development as an active and dynamic leader; you are also establishing the ongoing steps to build a stronger or enhanced connection with your team of associates.

As a manager and leader of your organization, you have a responsibility for properly utilizing human resources management skills with your associates. Your associates look to you for direction when it comes to appropriate training, education, and feedback. An all too common theme is the annual review and feedback. Most organizations have moved to help associates reach their potential by utilizing professional development plans. Even though this is an effective tool in writing down the goals, objectives, and ambitions of an associate, these plans and annual reviews have lost some of their value to staff, as well as managers.

Some may look at completing and discussing annual reviews as similar to completing your taxes annually. You know that it is going to happen, and often there is not much of a surprise at the conclusion of the forms. When discussing with other managers around performance review time, it is somewhat discouraging to hear that some view it as a chore. Sometimes they conclude with a raise, bonus, or some form of discussion; however, managers should understand the perspective of their associates.

As discussed earlier, you should understand the goals, ambitions, and motives of why your associates are coming to work. Ask yourself what purpose does working under your direction provide? Are you merely a means to the end, where the associate comes in, performs the tasks, and gets a paycheck every two weeks? Are you capturing the work and performance of your associates in a year's time, or whatever best comes to mind at that moment?

The answer to these questions is important as it helps paint a better picture of what the associate may be feeling the moment he or she walks through the door for the dreaded review. Although annual evaluations are necessary and part of human resources management, I recommend that you extend the feedback process throughout the entire year. You do not necessarily have to provide a form and sit down with an associate every three or six months; however, one thing to keep in mind is that the associates get the most extended one on one attention only during orientation and annual reviews.

Feedback is an important dynamic element of leadership. Too often, we focus on what is incorrect, rather than accentuating the positive. Under previous management thought processes, constructive criticism was popular. As previously emphasized throughout the book, today's worker is more complex than the past. As a result, your interactions with your associates during the feedback process should feature an ability to be in tune with the individual's personality.

One shoe does not fit all when it comes to leadership. You may have someone who is relatively quiet and may not need much involvement or interaction to perform at a high level. However, someone else under your guidance may require additional feedback or stimulation to achieve the essential functions of the job. The demographics of the modern worker dictates the need to become flexible and adapt to any subtle changes in the individual's persona.

Attempt to approach feedback objectively. Remove subjective thoughts or suggestions when providing feedback. Facts are difficult to dispute when presented correctly. Providing subjective feedback may backfire because you offer the individual a viewpoint generally viewed as biased. A good example includes the precise detail of the events that affected scoring criteria. If possible, try to notate issues that critically could have an impact on the organization positively or negatively objectively. Stating an error in providing a recommendation resulted in a loss of $34,000 is factual and provides more of a clearer picture of what happened. Indicating that poor decision making could have led to a claims loss does not provide a clearly stated result of the individual's action.

Despite some of the objective information provided in positive or negative feedback, providing a sense of belongingness or the opportunity to feel connected to the organizational culture should remain an objective of providing feedback. Some associates may state that they do not come to work to make friends; however, relationships are still formed and forged. Nurturing these bonds may improve communication and efficiency of operations.

The organizational culture is akin to family. Some family members get along great, and sometimes there will be dysfunction. Despite some quirkiness of the traits of some individuals, everyone is together, like family, to achieve his or her personal purposes. That individual's purpose helps achieve the wholeness of the organization. Because of this, providing feedback that helps promote growth is vital in the organizational culture.

When you are involved in a team, you will often either compromise or collaborate with your teammates. Collaboration requires the ability to work across boundaries. Collaboration includes the capacity to share resources. Emotional intelligence helps enhance collaboration in the context of leadership. By blending thoughts and feelings, as well as ideas, emotional intelligence provides an additional level of energy to improve collaboration.

Despite the amount of experience or knowledge in a particular industry, collaboration is a requirement among the team. With significant advances in technology and external environmental factors, collaboration is necessary as even the least experienced associate can provide significant value to the organization. Developing positive collaboration benefits all parties involved, especially if it is effectively positive.

Positive collaboration creates a synergistic bond. As a dynamic leader, you should continue to seek ways to collaborate or build with your associates whenever possible. Remember that your success correlates with the success of your team. You cannot be great unless those under your leadership are great. Seeking and continuing to nurture effective ways of creating positive collaboration should be an ongoing goal in leadership when the opportunity presents itself.

Optimism is contagious. If you are an optimistic person, innovative thinking and increased possibilities to overcome challenges may occur. Imagine the value of putting on the positive "game face" rather than the dour version. The way you walk into a facility or meeting projects not an aura of who you are as a person, but how others will feed off you during the duration of the day.

Leaving your problems behind has value. Everyone has their good days and down days. Some carry an additional level of stress or personal crises outside of work. Unfortunately, some people may bring their troubles to work. This statement holds true with those in management. Often when I conduct leadership or development training, I often scan the room and note the expressions of other people faces. My goal for the duration of the meeting or training is to engage that individual positively. Doing so may encourage the individal to provide valuable insight into the conversation. Sometimes, providing an opportunity for others to feel like they are part of a team pays dividends in the long run.

Collaboration is not easy. Sometimes there are barriers to collaboration. Often, the largest barrier to collaboration includes a lack of trust. Sometimes distrust may occur from unfamiliarity between parties; however, at times the actions displayed by one individual may sabotage any efforts to build any legitimate efforts to build on collaboration. If trust deficits do occur, your role as a leader is to re-establish a baseline and develop new boundaries that others may follow.

Trust is a fragile alliance between two parties that is susceptible to swings. Once you establish trust as a leader, it is imperative to nurture and maintain a high level of confidence. Once trust is violated, it is difficult to re-establish it. If trust is compromised, use your emotional intelligence to perform a root-cause analysis into what caused the breach of trust. From there, you must construct ways to connect with your associates on an emotional level before rebuilding trust completely.

Sometimes collaboration is negatively affected by personalized conflict. Even though the conflict does not involve you personally, the personalized conflict has the potential to become disruptive within the organizational culture or dynamic. As a dynamic leader, you should seek to root out the source of conflict and find ways to diffuse the situation before it grows from a disruptive force to a destructive force.

Optimal collaboration is constructed and not manufactured. High achieving teams and organizational relationships include individuals who feature interpersonal skills, shared motivation, and strong communication skills. Communication, which is a common theme throughout the *Four Fits* model, improves the likelihood of diffusing conflict and removing actual or perceived barriers within the team.

Building up others who follow your lead comes through successful coaching. Previously, we discussed feedback and collaboration concerning emotional intelligence. The third element of dynamic leadership in the context of emotional intelligence involves coaching. Throughout an associate's lifetime in the organizational culture, it is the leader's responsibility to ensure that the appropriate tools and resources are available and accessible.

Connecting with your team involves strong communication tools comprising of sending and receiving. Under the traditional communication model, sending and receiving help transmit or encodes messages between two parties. Concerning coaching using emotional intelligence, you utilize these tools to motivate, lead, inspire, as well as listen. Sometimes a leader's ability to listen could be skewed by preconceived bias or assumptions of a particular person or situation. The barriers caused by doing so may limit your ability to coach an individual to excellence.

Despite your accomplishments and achievements, it can be difficult at times to hear the voices of those who are under your charge. At times, obsessing over the success or numerical goals may tune out the wants or needs of the employees who may negatively affect operational efficiency. An example of this includes an account manager who is laser-focused on reaching her metrics but not taking the time to perform a root-cause analysis on the underlying problems persistent in her account.

As a safety and risk manager, I recall how important it was to achieve statistical goals such as reducing claim costs and total claims by 5-10%, among other desirable metrics. When I first came aboard, it was somewhat overwhelming, not because I did not have the technical knowledge of the industry; it was due to not being able to connect with my team. I spent the first year or so locked in trying to reach my metrics; however, I did not spend too much time developing an understanding as to why the numbers existed. Once I was able to listen more effectively and learned how to connect to my team, reductions exceeded expectations.

Throughout this book, I mention an ability to connect with the team or an individual. Emotional intelligence involves self-awareness and self-management among other characteristics. If you are connected to your self-awareness, you would demonstrate an ability to become a more active and avid listener. Even though our attention spans diminished over time due to smartphones, emails, text messaging, and other electronic methods of distracting us, take the time to coach and lead your team to involve several traits discussed below.

Patience, or lack thereof, sends a message to your associate who is attempting to communicate with you. Cutting off someone or trying to finish someone else's sentence sends a message that you are not genuinely interested in what the other person has to say. Another way to show poor listening skills or showing disinterest in your team involves trying to be right rather than trying to recognize value in another person's opinion.

I recall a manager who I often counseled privately. An apparent discord occurred between her team and herself. When we discussed possible causes of this dispute, I advised that some of the issues started with her and her method of not listening. Naturally, she became offended and defensive. I pointed out to her that everything from body language, facial expressions, and the tone of voice used in response sends a negative message to her team. As a result, her team did not respond well when challenged. It was more interesting to note that even though the tone was not critical, the same traits I observed in her team she demonstrated to me. I pointed out that 85% of communication is said to be non-verbal, and to better lead her team, she would benefit the team by being cognizant of such mannerisms.

Becoming self-aware is difficult. Equate self-awareness to an out-of-body experience such as a sci-fi or cartoon where your astral form is looking at your physical form. Key in on the non-verbal responses provided by the receiver of the message given. If you see your associate reacting in a negative fashion, it is likely that you may not have clearly communicated or provided counsel in a manner conducive to the situation.

If you are not completely self-aware now, achieving this state of mind will take some time. I often liken it to one of the axioms previously provided under the Mental Fit of slowing the tone, pace, and tempo down. Too often when engaging another party, we find ourselves quick to rush to judgment or formulate an inaccurate opinion because, in our mind, we feel that we either know the answer or assume that the other person does not understand the topic.

Empathy is a trait under emotional intelligence that can enhance coaching skills. Understanding the desires and needs of those under your leadership help provide opportunities for improvement and education to fill in the gaps in an individual's performance. Despite the talent that resides in your associates, your unstated purpose of your position involves the ability to bring out the best in others.

Research shows the value of empathy. The Center for Creative Leadership recommended that leaders need to become more person-focused and show followers that they care (Gentry, Weber, & Sadri, 2011). Relating to your employees and displaying genuine compassion towards others provide connectivity and improve overall performance. Demonstrating empathy shows compassion and your ability to be an active listener.

Active listening provides benefits to leaders. Picking up on non-verbal cues including tone, facial expressions, body language, and eye movement assists an active listener in understanding the deeper extent or context provided by the other party. As an active listener, additional opportunities exist by asking or probing deeper into a situation that needs resolution. If a situation existed where you, as a leader, must make a critical decision, that decision is made much easier as an active listener.

Processing relative information that is critical to the organization or resolving conflict is a benefit derived from active listening. The practice of this particular style of thinking allows you to slow everything down to the point where you capable of receiving and processing the necessary information to enhance your decision-making capabilities. Often as leaders, we are far removed from the floor or field activities. Interactions have more of a political feel to it, and perceived barriers exist between the associates and management. Staff holds vital information that provides an enhanced value to the organization and strategy development. Therefore, the combination of empathy and active listening creates additional opportunities that could benefit all parties involved.

In the final exercise for this book, Worksheet #10, the focus will be your ability to relate and understand your emotional intelligence. Within this axiom, the three areas of emotional intelligence discussed in this book included feedback, collaboration, and coaching. Connecting to your associates is connecting to your base. If you do not make a connection with your associates, your message becomes diluted, and at times, lost. Developing and executing active leadership is akin to gardening or landscaping. The growth and overall outlook during the warmer months mirror the amount of effort and energy you expend towards it. This analogy holds true in your ability to become an effective and active leader. The more energy and effort you put in your team, using your emotional intelligence, the likelier overall productivity, engagement, and buy-in increases.

CONCLUSION

LEADERSHIP IS ALWAYS in a state of evolution and growth, requiring those in key positions to adapt to their environment continuously. Such challenges derive from internal and external stakeholders as well as the organizational culture. Today's employee features more empowerment and a sense of independence, as well as some form of entitlement. Today's workers are relatively more intelligent and have access to numerous resources to empower them to make decisions that may affect the direction of the organization.

The major challenge for those in critical positions involves the ability to develop a more dynamic and interactive leadership style. Organizations are more prone to turnover due to the instability of workers seeking to maximize their financial and personal benefits. Due to the lack of corporate loyalty, leadership must understand their associates and develop ways to remain connected to them as well as fulfill the organization's vision and mission. Becoming disengaged from those who are under your guidance is a quick way to guarantee lower employee morale, lack of employee engagement, as well as increase overall turnover rates.

Resistance to change is a natural phenomenon for associates when confronted with new demands, processes, and changes to their overall routine. Understanding the cause of associate angst, while still holding firm to the objectives set forth provides you a stronger outlook into developing ways of administering your leadership style. Ignoring why there is resistance to change or believing that this phenomenon does not exist could create challenges in innovation, customer service, and buy-in to the overall organizational culture.

The Four Fits of Dynamic Leadership focuses on a general theme, your ability to become dynamic, flexible, and connected to your staff, as well as developing an enhanced understanding of who you are as a person and leader. Establishing this connectivity comes from understanding the more human qualities of your personality, and utilizing your soft skills to remain engaged with your team. Rather than viewing a leadership style within a matrix, expand your leadership style to think more outside the box. The philosophy of *The Four Fits* is to expand what you know through a combination of education, experience, and mentoring into a more nuanced and subtle means of thinking.

The Four Fits of Dynamic Leadership is a philosophy developed to help current and future leaders of the 21st century. As we continue to be immersed in numerous information, technological advances, social media, and the ever-changing psyche of the average employee, flexibility and a willingness to adapt increase the chances of greater viability within the industry, as well as creating a new competitive advantage against industry competitors. Everyone is now a critic, and there are numerous media available to provide an opinion that could negatively affect the overall image of the organization. Although there are not many articles discussing the overall effect of material posted online about an organization, it is reasonable to believe that a healthy percentage of incoming and current associates have a perception that is unhealthy and negative.

Expanding traditional and more commonly discussed management and leadership concepts, *The Four Fits* breaks the traditional matrix model into a more open and fluid frame of thinking and engagement. Within this open design are the four respective Fits: Mental, Emotional, Team, and Personal Power. Each of these Fits was designed to interact within the sphere; thus creating the ability for a leader to combine the Fits in a given situation or encounter. The removing of the lines or barriers as seen in a matrix model provides an opportunity to promote originality and freedom in the leader's mentality, as well as to keep an individual confined within a box or defined as a particular type of leader or learner. Thus, the emphasis throughout this book on the word "dynamic," as each one of you is dynamic and brings different qualities to the table. I encourage you to let your personality grow, and allow others to follow your lead.

THE FOUR FITS OF DYNAMIC LEADERSHIP WORKSHEETS AND EXERCISES

"BE DYNAMIC, BE REFLECTIVE, BE YOU!!!"

——— ⌒ ———

DICTATING THE TONE, PACE, AND TEMPO OF YOUR ENVIRONMENT

IN LEADERSHIP, YOU will encounter challenges that may distort or distract you from your vision. As a dynamic leader, the challenge is to recognize the situation or challenge you are facing and to determine a way or method to slow things down. Being sped up in your mind leads to an increase in mental errors in judgement. In this exercise, think of different scenarios where you may have been thrown off balance, but sought ways to create balance. Feel free to utilize a scenario that you may not have been personally involved in, but thought how you could have addressed it differently:

Scenario 1:

_____

_____

Tone (Actual/How did you address the tone?):

_____

_____

Pace (Actual/How did you achieve the pace?):

_____

_____

Tempo (Actual/How did you change the tempo?):

_____

_____

Scenario 2:

_____

_____

Tone (Actual/How did you address the tone?):

_____

_____

Pace (Actual/How did you achieve the pace?):

_____

_____

Tempo (Actual/How did you change the tempo?):

_____

_____

How Do You Rate Your Three C's

Under Axiom #2, we explored the three C's: Clarity, Commitment, and Communication. Utilizing this model, do you have balance within these three areas? Do you find yourself struggling in certain areas more than others? What areas do you feel like you can improve? In this exercise, discuss your strengths, challenges, and areas of opportunities, and what you could do to enhance your 3 C's.

Clarity:

My strengths:

_____

_____

Challenges:

_____

_____

Opportunities:

_____

_____

Communication:

My strengths:

_____

_____

Challenges:

_____

_____

Opportunities:

_____

_____

Commitment:

My strengths:

_____

_____

Challenges:

_____

_____

Opportunities:

_____

_____

ADJUST, ADAPT, AND MOVE FORWARD

THE WORKPLACE FEATURES a unique and ever-changing environment where there are rarely two days that are the same. Most industries are now geared to service-oriented industries where interactions between the organization and stakeholders have grown. This evolution of relationships provides more variables and challenges wherein management must demonstrate an ability to adjust, adapt, and move forward. In this exercise, identify three situations where you had to adjust, adapt, and move forward. After identifying these situations, document your lessons learned from each situation you encountered.

Scenario 1:

_____

_____

Adjust:

_____

_____

Adapt:

_____

_____

Moving Forward:

_____

_____

Lessons Learned:

_____

_____

Scenario 2:

_____

_____

Adjust:

_____

_____

Adapt:

_____

_____

Lessons Learned:

_____

_____

Scenario 3:

_____

_____

Adjust:

_____

_____

Adapt:

_____

_____

Moving Forward:

_____

_____

Lessons Learned:

_____

_____

YOUR JOURNEY TO GREATNESS BEGAN WHEN...

EVERY STORY HAS a beginning, middle, and end. Some who are reading this book and completing the related worksheets may be further along in their career than others. Despite whatever stage you are currently in your professional career, there was a beginning and a pivotal moment that has helped shape you into the individual that you are today. These same flashpoints are critical in your development for your future development as well. For this exercise, identify your humble beginnings and a pivotal moment in your professional (or personal) life that helped guide you today.

In the beginning, I…:

_____

_____

The moment of clarity in my professional/personal life was when…..:

_____

_____

What I learned from those experiences helped shape me to be the person I am today because:

_____

_____

UNDERSTAND AND EMBRACE YOUR WORK-LIFE BALANCE

ESTABLISHING AND MAINTAINING a healthy work-life balance is important for your mental, emotional, and physical well-being. Being too engrossed with your responsibilities will create burnout and possible health concerns. In this exercise, think about five hobbies you enjoy. If you do not have five hobbies, now will be a good time to think about what exactly you enjoy and make it a point to partake in those activities from time to time. Next to your hobbies, indicate how often you participate in each of them.

Hobby #1:

_____

Hobby #2:

_____

Hobby #3:

_____

Hobby #4:

_____

Hobby #5:

_____

THE CAUSE AND EFFECT FROM YOUR LEADERSHIP STYLE

As a LEADER, you decisions affect your external and internal stakeholders. At times, those decisions may motivate others to improve efficiencies in work performance. Conversely, those decisions may result in negative morale, misunderstanding of the intended message, and confusion. In this exercise, discuss three situations or scenarios where there were a significant cause-and-effect based on your decision-making in a leadership or professional environment. Document lessons learned from these events, and outline what you may do differently in encountering a similar situation in the future.

Scenario 1:

_____

_____

Cause:

_____

_____

Effect:

_____

_____

Lessons Learned:

_____

_____

Scenario 2:

_____

_____

Cause:

_____

_____

Effect:

_____

_____

Lessons Learned:

_____

_____

Scenario 3:

_____

_____

Cause:

_____

_____

Effect:

_____

_____

Lessons Learned:

_____

_____

LEADERSHIP BY EXAMPLE: TO BE SEEN AND HEARD

YOUR STYLE OF leadership should always evolve with the make-up of your staff. To have others adapt or follow your vision, consider how often you are visible to your team. Even if you have a high level of visibility, you should continue to demonstrate effective two-way communication between your staff and yourself. Developing the appropriate synergy with your team includes your ability not only to be seen, but how vocal and connected you are to all of your stakeholders. In this exercise, in your opinion, rate your level of visibility and communication to your team. Contemplate what you could do to improve or enhance both areas.

_____

_____

_____

_____

_____

_____

_____

_____

THERE IS NO "I" IN TEAM

IN THIS EXERCISE, you are asked to evaluate your relationship with your associates, or those who work under your supervision, or those who report directly to you. We often are in the business of evaluating the talent of others; however, how often do we assess ourselves as leaders. This particular exercise provides you the opportunity to take a step back as to how you rate yourself as a leader, identify your strengths and opportunities for improvement. If you are completing this exercise on your own, do not be afraid to solicit input from your team. Remember the better you are as a leader, the more of a positive impact you have on those following your lead.

Communication of Goals, Objectives, and Mission of the Organization

_____

_____

Active Listening (Providing constructive feedback without references of personal traits)

_____

_____

Accessibility (Open door policy, team feels comfortable speaking freely)

_____

_____

Collaboration (Demonstrating a willingness to allow others take an active lead in development of strategy)

_____

_____

Policy Hawk or Reasonable to Real-Life Events (How strict do you follow policy)

_____

_____

Overall Leadership Style

_____

_____

WHAT ARE YOUR CHARACTERISTICS OF GREATNESS

ESTABLISHING AND MAINTAINING a healthy relationship with your associates comes from your ability to develop a strong team dynamic. In this exercise, identify what you feel are your tangible and intangible traits that contribute towards your leadership style. After you doing so, research two characteristics that you feel could compliment your current attributes, and comment on how you can incorporate them into your persona as a dynamic leader.

My Intangible Characteristics

_____

_____

My Tangible Characteristics

_____

_____

Additional intangible characteristics I can incorporate (identify why this is important to your overall professional growth).

_____

_____

Additional tangible characteristics I can incorporate (identify why this is important to your overall professional growth).

_____

_____

EMOTIONAL INTELLIGENCE

EMOTIONAL INTELLIGENCE COMES from the capacity to become empathetic and understand how to recognize and effectively label the emotions or feelings of another. Establishing, nurturing, and maintain a relationship with your associates comes from your ability to connect. The combination of active listening and empathy increases your awareness in three areas discussed in the book: feedback, collaboration, and coaching. For this exercise, rate where you feel you currently are among the three areas. After rating, discuss ways that you can enhance your emotional intelligence in these three areas.

Feedback

1   2   3   4   5

How can I improve providing feedback for those under my leadership:

_____

_____

Collaboration

1   2   3   4   5

How can I enhance collaboration within the team:

_____

_____

Coaching

1   2   3   4   5

How effective is my current coaching style. I can improve by performing the following:

_____

_____

REFERENCES

Briggs, S. (2014). How empathy affects learning, and how to cultivate it in your students [Blog]. *InformEd*. Retrieved from http://www. opencolleges.edu.au/informed/features/empathy-and-learning/

Bureau of Labor Statistics. (2016). *Employee Tenure in 2016* [Press release]. Retrieved from HYPERLINK "https://www.bls.gov/news.release/ tenure.nr0.htm" https://www.bls.gov/news.release/tenure.nr0.htm

Duncan, T. (2016). *The Four Fits of Holistic Growth*. North Charleston, S.C., Createspace Independent Publishing Platform.

Flauto, F. (1999). Walking the Talk: The Relationship Between Leadership and Communication Competence. *Journal of Leadership and Organizational Studies*, 86-97. doi:10.1177/107179199900600106

Freeman, R. (1984). Strategic Management: A stakeholder approach. Boston: Pittman.

Gentry, W. A., Weber, T. J., & Sadri, G. (2011). *Empathy in the workplace*. Center for Creative Leadership. Retrieved from http://www.ccl.org/ wp-content/uploads/2015/04/EmpathyInTheWorkplace.pdf

Giles, S. (2016). The most important leadership competencies, according to leaders. *Harvard Business Review.*

Green, R. (1999). Leadership as a function of power. *Proposal Management*, 34 - 53.

Groysberg, B., & Abrahams, R. (2014). *ww.hbr.org*. Retrieved from Harvard Business Review: https://hbr.org/2014/03/manage-your-work-manage-your-life

Hackman, M. Z., & Johnson, C. E. (2004). *Leadership: A communication perspective*. Long Grove, Ill: Waveland Press.

Heremuru, C. (2008). *Ezine Articles.* Retrieved from http://ezinearticles. com/?A-Symbiotic-Relationship-Between-Leaders-and-Followers&id=1299700

Laschinger, H.K., Wong, C.A., & Greco, P. (2006). The impact of staff nurse empowerment on person-job fit and work engagement/burnout. *Nurse Administration Quarterly, 30(4),* 358-367. Retrieved from https://www.ncbi.nlm.nih.gov/pubmed/17077717

Meyers, S. (2013). *Definition of Team Dynamics.* Retrieved from www. teamtechnology.co.uk: http://www.teamtechnology.co.uk/team/ dynamics/definition/

Ovans, A. (2015). *Harvard Business Review.* Retrieved from www.hbr.org: https://hbr.og/2015/04/how-emotional-intelligence-became-a-key-leadership-skill

Patel, V., Dhopeshwarkar, R., Edwards, A., Barron, Y., Sparenborg, J., & Kaushal, R. (2012). Consumer support for health information exchange and personal health records: A regional health information organization survey. *Journal of Medical Systems, 36,* 1043-1052. doi:10.1007/s10916-010-9566-0

Plsek, P.E., & Wilson, T. (2001). Complexity, leadership, and management in healthcare organisations. *British Medical Journal, 323(7315),* 746-749. Retrieved from https://www.ncbi.nlm.nih.gov/pmc/articles/ PMC1121291/

Schuler, A. (2003). *Overcoming Resistance to Change: Top Ten Reasons for Change Resistance.* Retrieved from uthscsa.edu: http://uthscsa.edu/ gme/documents/chiefres/Change%20Leadership/Overcoming%20 Resistance%20to%20Change.pdf

West, M.A., Borill, C.S., Dawson, J.F., Brodbeck, F., Shapiro, D.A., & Haward, B. (2003). Leadership clarity and team innovation in health care. *The Leadership Quarterly, 14,* 393 – 410. doi: 10.1016/ S1048-9843(03)00044-4

Made in the USA
Middletown, DE
09 September 2021

47869517R00076